More Praise for
The Uncluttered Heart

OPENING THE PAGES OF THIS BOOK is like entering a holy place. You meet wise teachers through their quotes, comforting and challenging biblical texts, simple words for your pocket, prayers for the heart, and Beth who weaves it all together with her own story, so we can approach the manger with an uncluttered heart—and kneel.

—LARRY J. PEACOCK
Executive Director, Rolling Ridge Retreat and Conference Center
North Andover, Massachusetts
Author, *Openings: A Daybook of Saints, Psalms, and Prayer*

The Uncluttered Heart

Making Room for God During Advent and Christmas

UPPER
ROOM BOOKS®
NASHVILLE

beth a. richardson

Cover design: Micah Kandross
Cover image: istock.com
First printing: 2009

LIBRARY OF CONGRESS CATALOGING-IN-PUBLICATION DATA

Richardson, Beth A.
   The uncluttered heart: making room for God during Advent and Christmas / Beth A. Richardson.
      p. cm.
   ISBN 978-0-8358-9994-9
   1. Advent—Prayers and devotions. 2. Christmas—Prayers and devotions. 3. Epiphany—Prayers and devotions. I. Title.
   BV40.R523 2009
   242'.33—dc22   2009001792

Printed in the United States of America

To

Jenni

Contents

Advent . . .

marks the beginning of the church year and lays before us the pathway of faith for the year ahead. Advent initiates once again remembering, retelling, and celebrating the whole drama of God's revelation.

Four weeks is the limit to this season that declares the truth about a God whose love and resourcefulness have no limits. "Advent" has its roots in the Latin word *adventus*, or coming. This season proclaims the coming of Christ in the birth of Jesus, in the Word and Spirit, and in the final victory when God's kingdom shall be complete. *Our privilege* as Christians is to receive the gracious gifts of God's presence in Christ. *Our task* is to prepare for his coming so that we will not miss life's greatest gift.

—Norman Shawchuck and Rueben P. Job
A Guide to Prayer for All Who Seek God

Acknowledgments

I JOINED THE UPPER ROOM MINISTRIES staff shortly after graduating from divinity school. I took a job as an assistant editor at *Alive Now* magazine. It was the best job in the universe, as far as I was concerned. Under the guidance of my colleagues, Mary Ruth Coffman and Deen Thompson, I learned about editing, writing, the church year, designated scripture readings, local church work, and how to teach the Christian faith. Through the next many years, the staff and culture of The Upper Room nurtured me in my spiritual life, shaping me, in many ways, into the person I have become. I'm very grateful for this tremendous opportunity to work, to shape and be shaped by the amazing staff who make up this important ministry. Further, I'm thankful for the opportunity to write about Advent and how to survive its perils without losing all sense of the spiritual. Many thanks to Robin Pippin for inviting me into this adventure and to Rita Collett for editing the book.

To all my Upper Room colleagues, I love you, and I'm grateful for your continuing influence on my daily life and spiritual journey.

—Fall 2008

Introduction

Everywhere and always God is with us, near to us and in us. But we are not always with [God], since we do not remember [God]....Take upon yourself this task—to make a habit of such recollection. Make yourself a rule always to be with the Lord, keeping your mind in your heart, and do not let your thoughts wander; as often as they stray, turn them back again and keep them at home in the closet of your heart, and delight in converse with the Lord.

—Saint Theophan the Recluse
The Art of Prayer

I'VE ALWAYS LOVED ADVENT. Growing up in a Methodist preacher's household, I experienced Advent in family celebrations led by my parents. These celebrations at home—lighting the candles on our Advent wreath and having a family devotional time each Sunday evening—shaped my love of the season. I didn't know *why* we observed Advent. It was just part of our family tradition. All family members participated weekly according to our gifts. When each child turned five or so, he or she got to light the candles on the Advent wreath (the favorite childhood activity). When we learned to read, we shared the leadership of our family observance by reading the scripture or devotional for that day. Mom and Dad—and later, each of the children—took turns leading the singing of the hymn for that week or accompanying the hymn on piano. For several years we used an Advent wreath and nativity scene Dad had made out of copper wire.

Working here at Upper Room Ministries, I learned the *why* of Advent. I became aware that rituals of preparation—just like in our daily lives—preceded special events in the Christian life. I wouldn't invite people over for dinner without cleaning the house. And I ready myself for the birth of Christ by getting rid of the clutter in my heart. Advent is about making room in my life—my heart, mind, and spirit—for God's blessing through Jesus' birth. When that holy day comes, I want to have a spacious heart ready for God's gift of love.

I've lived out my love of Advent in my work life, first through writing litanies and prayers for *Alive Now* magazine and then through the creation of online Advent devotionals for Upper Room Ministries' Web presence. In these online resources, each day features a short quote from an Upper Room book.

My first Advent book for Upper Room Books, *Child of the Light*, culminated my lifetime love of Advent in a special way. When Upper Room Books approached me to contribute another Advent book, I was honored. In this book, my love of Advent joins with my work in the Web ministry. I've gone back through the years of selections we have used in our Advent Web resources and have picked out some of my favorite quotes to use each day during Advent and the Christmas season that follows. Many of these quotes feel like old friends, and I'm glad to introduce you to them.

Some of this book's concepts are rooted in the desert tradition of the Christian church. In ancient times, the abbas and ammas (fathers and mothers) of Egyptian monasticism made their home in the desert, alone in hermitages or gathered in communities. Their experiences of living alone or in community, facing temptation, and learning to live in God's grace became the roots of the monastic movements of later centuries. Recountings of their experiences developed into a body of stories from the desert fathers and mothers. The concept of remembering God through the day comes from this ancient tradition. Also from this tradition comes the daily element in this book: receiving a word or phrase to carry with you into the day. Pilgrims would come to the ammas and abbas and ask, "Give me a word of life." So, at the end of each reflection, I give a few words to carry through the day.

We come hungry to this season of preparation—hungry for words of life, for rituals of preparation, for disciplines to help us on our way. Remember God. Receive words of life. Walk with one another into the days of Advent.

PURPOSE OF THE BOOK

Advent is the season of the church year during which we prepare our lives—our hearts, minds, and spirits—for the coming of the Christ child. During these four weeks preceding Christmas, we prepare our "outside lives." We buy gifts, make family plans, attend special church services, and clean house. We also prepare our hearts, minds, and spirits by sweeping out the corners of our hearts, cleaning up the clutter in order to make space for God's hope, peace, joy, love, and presence.

Advent is often the busiest time of the year. And yet, we are called to make time and space to prepare our hearts for the coming of Christ. What a challenge for us as Christians. This book's purpose resides in helping us clear away obstructions to God—our worries, distractions, negative habits—so that our hearts and spirits are open to God's movement during this holy time. No matter how busy we may become, God is waiting to break through our endless tasks and distractions to remind us that we are not alone; indeed, God is present with us in every moment.

Christian spirituality focuses on helping us remember God throughout our day. From Paul's exhorting the Thessalonians to "pray without ceasing" (1 Thess. 5:17) to Brother Lawrence's practicing the presence of God in each daily task, we are challenged and encouraged to connect with God—to remember God—not just during formal worship or daily meditation time but throughout the day. Theophan the Recluse exhorts us to remember God: "Make yourself a rule always to be with the Lord, keeping your mind in your heart, and do not let your thoughts wander; as often as they stray, turn them back again and keep them at home in the closet of your heart, and delight in converse with the Lord." We need not get discouraged if remembering God through the day is difficult. This practice is a skill to be developed over time, a practice learned over a lifetime.

During the coming Advent and Christmas season, I invite you to remember God as much as you can; in doing so, you will maintain a true center during this holy time. Carry one of the elements from each day's reflection with you into the day. You may copy a particular day's quote or scripture reading to put in your worship space, on your desk, or in your calendar.

Sign up at unclutteredheart.org to receive a daily electronic reminder of each day's theme. The daily text message or e-mail will remind you to pause a moment for your spirit during the busy day. Register and "remember God" during the time you use this book.

At any time in the day, take a break and remind yourself of God's presence. Meditate on the theme for the current week or the phrase for that day. Say a prayer. Or just pause and create silent space inside of you. Feel God's love filling you. Remember God when you see a child laughing or witness a stranger's kindness to another. Remember God when you hear tragic news or observe a friend's sadness. Remember God when surrounded by a crowd, sitting alone, or lying in bed in the quiet of early morning. Remember God when you check your e-mail or when you receive a text message. *Remember God.* God is there, waiting for you to remember.

USING THE BOOK

This book may be used by an individual or a group. Each day's meditation stands alone as an invitation to the reader to stop and connect with God for that moment and then later during the day.

A group study guide offers suggestions for using the book as the focal point of four Advent gatherings. Also at the end of the book you will find four Advent litanies and a litany for Christmas Eve or Christmas Day. They may be used in your congregation's corporate worship or in your family worship during Advent and Christmas.

Advent begins four weeks before Christmas and ends with Christmas Eve. I wrote this book to accommodate any year of Advent, so you may not need all the meditations written for the fourth week.

Each week of Advent features a traditional theme used across the church: hope (week 1), peace (week 2), joy (week 3), and love (week 4). Beginning Christmas Day, the theme for the rest of the book is presence. The meditations continue through the twelve days of Christmas and the day of Epiphany (January 6). I encourage your pursuit of study past Christmas Day so you have the time and space to celebrate Christ's coming and be open to God's movement in your life during this time of presence.

Each day's meditation contains the following items: a quote from an Upper Room book, a short scripture, a reflection and prayer written by me, and a short sentence or phrase that sums up the theme for each day. If you remember nothing else from the day's reading, carry the phrase with you throughout the day.

At the end of the book, you'll find a group study guide. Although you can use this resource by yourself, I encourage you to find a way to join with others during this time. The members of your Sunday school class or Wednesday night gathering may want to covenant to use the book during Advent and Christmas. If you don't have such a group to join with, I encourage you to find at least one other person who will read the book with you. In this way, you will receive and give support during your Advent journey.

Sign up to receive a daily electronic reminder of each day's theme. The daily text message or e-mail will remind you to pause a moment for your spirit during the busy days of Advent and Christmas.

unclutteredheart.org

First Week of Advent: Hope

Sunday

God of . . . darkness and Christmas light. . . . Deepen my longing, heighten my expectation, and make pregnant my hope. I know that within my heart is a Bethlehem: a place where light shines with tender memories. A place where angelic voices sing loud and clear. A place of wonder and awe, delight and calm. . . . God of . . . darkness and Christmas light, journey with me during these days so that I may know and prize my Bethlehem moments. Amen.

—Larry James Peacock
Openings

SCRIPTURE

The days are surely coming, says the LORD, when I will fulfill the promise I made to the house of Israel and the house of Judah. In those days and at that time I will cause a righteous Branch to spring up for David; and he shall execute justice and righteousness in the land. In those days Judah will be saved and Jerusalem will live in safety. And this is the name by which it will be called: "The LORD is our righteousness."

—Jeremiah 33:14-16

REFLECTION

The first candle on the Advent wreath is the candle of hope. When we light the candle of hope—in the Advent wreath or in our hearts—we kindle a flame of expectant anticipation that something rich, something special, is on its way.

As we enter into this Advent journey, we already know that the something special at the end of Advent is the birth of Christ,

God's great gift to the world. But much of the richness of this season comes with the anticipation, the waiting, the deferral of the celebration until the appropriate time.

During Advent, the first season of the church year, we relive the story of Jesus, the wonder of how he came to be, the story of his birth. We don't yet know what God has in store, but we trust God's promises of righteousness, justice, and peace for our hurting world and our discouraged spirits. We live in the hope, that despite our current struggles, God has something good in store for us.

Jesus, the hope of the world, is coming to an unsuspecting world.

God of Advent, kindle within me the flame of hope. As I walk through this day, may that hope remind me of your promise that something good is coming. Amen.

CARRY THESE WORDS IN YOUR HEART TODAY
Deepen my longing for you, O God.

Monday

John the Baptist is the Advent adventurer, stalking through the wilderness of his time on the trail of the messiah. He's the original hellfire-and-brimstone preacher, but he also offers hope to the community he rakes over the coals. A willingness to hope is a willingness to enter the wilderness. Hope is not a domesticated state of mind. It seems to camp out in odd places, crops up at the worst possible times. Just as we resign ourselves to the minimum wages of life with no benefits, hope whispers that we shouldn't settle for despair's bottom line. Hope thrives in the barren places of our lives.

—Heather Murray Elkins
The Upper Room Disciplines 2006

SCRIPTURE

In those days John the Baptist appeared in the wilderness of Judea, proclaiming, "Repent, for the kingdom of heaven has come near." This is the one of whom the prophet Isaiah spoke when he said,
"The voice of one crying out in the wilderness:
'Prepare the way of the Lord,
make his paths straight.'"

—Matthew 3:1-3

REFLECTION

As an Advent proponent, I love John the Baptist—at least from afar. (I'm not sure I would have been comfortable hanging out with a locust-eating, camel-hair-wearing prophet.) But John the Baptist's message to us during this frantic season of the year draws me in. I mean, here's this guy out in the wilderness proclaiming God's word, "Prepare the way of the Lord, make his paths straight." Who wants to hear the word *repent*? And who wants the extra work of making paths straight and all?

Yet we Advent journeyers also find ourselves in a sort of wilderness, a wilderness of excess, of noise and clutter and busyness; a wilderness of secular, consumer culture giving us the message that Christmas will be perfect if we buy the right presents—and do it now. We Advent people are crying out in this wilderness, trying to prepare the way in our own lives, trying to make a place, a holy space for the coming of the Christ child. We are called to prepare the way in the wilderness of pre-Christmas chaos, where rushed schedules and commercial chatter drown out silence and prayers.

And hope goes with us, *is with us*, in this wilderness of chaos. Hope becomes a critical part of our Advent survival kit, guiding us through the distractions, reminding us of our single task: to prepare the way.

God of hope, help me prepare the way for you in the wilderness of chaos. Give me strength, wisdom, and patience to clear a path for you through my cluttered heart and life. Amen.

Carry these words in your heart today

Hope thrives in the wilderness.

Tuesday

We may be surprised . . . that when we first enter into this "holy nothing" [silence], we initially encounter not God but ourselves—our own fears and uncertainties, our own projects, habits, hopes, and fears. Meeting our "self" in this way is difficult, and we must learn to sit with these obstacles as we become still so that we may know that God is God.

—Daniel Wolpert
Leading a Life with God

SCRIPTURE

"Come, let us go up to the mountain of the LORD,
    to the house of the God of Jacob;
that he may teach us his ways
    and that we may walk in his paths."
For out of Zion shall go forth instruction,
    and the word of the LORD from Jerusalem.
He shall judge between the nations,
    and shall arbitrate for many peoples;
they shall beat their swords into plowshares,
    and their spears into pruning hooks;
nation shall not lift up sword against nation,
    neither shall they learn war any more.

—Isaiah 2:3-4

REFLECTION

A number of years ago I was involved in the birth of a spiritual retreat center outside of Nashville, Tennessee. Part of this birthing work required a long process of community discernment. Those of us interested in the creation of a retreat center listened for what God was calling forth. We held quiet days, clearness committees, and retreats to assist us in our listening to the Spirit. An important part of the process came in blocks of time committed to silence. We went into times of silence—sometimes sitting together as a group and sometimes alone, walking on the land or finding a quiet place to listen.

Being young in the spiritual life, I had never been invited to be silent with God. I found at first that my brain chattered louder during the silent times than when I engaged in conversation. Whenever I entered a period of silence, a wave of thoughts and emotions tended to drown out anything God might be wanting to say to me. But over time, I got better at this spiritual practice. Each time I entered silence, I reached the quiet place quicker. I began to long for the peace that came once I had gotten past all the distractions. It just took practice.

This kind of listening to God's voice has now become a helpful Advent practice for me. During the busyness and chatter of this season of the year, I can carve out space and time to sit in silence, quiet my inner noise, and turn toward God. I don't necessarily need to spend hours in silence—minutes will do. Whenever I feel overwhelmed and speeded up, I turn my attention inward, close my ears to outward noise, take some deep breaths, and sink down into the welcoming silence of the heart of God.

I invite you to be silent with God today. Take five, ten, or fifteen minutes to be still in God's presence. Don't worry if you are not successful during the first try. This discipline grows with practice. Keep carving out some space during each day. Have hope; God is there, waiting for you.

God of stillness, it's easy to overlook you in these busy days. Create in me a longing for your quiet presence, that I may stop, breathe, and listen for your wisdom and instruction. Amen.

CARRY THESE WORDS IN YOUR HEART TODAY

God waits for me in the stillness.

Wednesday

Many demands upon our time and many opportunities waiting to be explored often fill our lives too full with activities and distractions. When this happens it is not surprising that we grow anxious and lose our sense of peace and tranquility. Today remember that God and God alone is able to care for all that exists; we can trust our smallest and largest concern to the wisdom and love of God. Peace, hope, calm, and joy are the fruits of placing our confidence in God. May these gifts be yours in abundance.

—Rueben P. Job
A Guide to Prayer for All Who Seek God

SCRIPTURE

It is now the moment for you to wake from sleep. For salvation is nearer to us now than when we became believers; the night is far gone, the day is near. Let us then lay aside the works of darkness and put on the armor of light.

—Romans 13:11-12

REFLECTION

I am easily hijacked by distractions, obsessions, and anxieties. It doesn't take much to knock me off my center and start me worrying. Worry and anxiety often seem to be my default response to any situation. When I am faced with change, unexpected turns in the road, or even small victories, my automatic response is worry.

Intellectually I acknowledge an appropriate choice of action: stop, pray, and trust God. But most of the time I forget these basic steps that restore my balance. When I find myself in turmoil, I often call a spiritual friend of mine. I recount my situation in detail with all its twists and turns. After I've completed my tale, my monologue finally comes to a halt. I hear silence on the other end of the phone, and then my friend asks, "Did you pray?" Usually I respond with a chuckle and a sheepish, "No, I forgot." "Okay, you know what to do," she says.

And I do know what to do: (1) Stop what I'm doing and turn my attention to God. (2) Pray. Turn over to God everything that is bothering me. (3) Trust God. Trust that no matter how difficult the situation, God will guide me.

Loving God, be patient when I stray from you, when I fail to turn to you during challenging times. Help me remember the simple things I can do to return from chaos to hope, peace, and serenity. For you are able to care for all that exists. Amen.

CARRY THESE WORDS IN YOUR HEART TODAY
I can trust my smallest concern to God's wisdom.

Thursday

For too many in this season of Advent, the future holds little hope or promise. The death of a loved one, estrangement within family, depression, illness: any or all of these issues can conspire to close off life from its possibilities. Before repentance can be sounded, comfort must be given. Comfort my people, says your God. Speak tenderly to Jerusalem.

That comfort also bears Advent's word of preparation. It declares that hope is still possible. It affirms that grace still awaits.

—John Indermark
Setting the Christmas Stage

SCRIPTURE

To you, O LORD, I lift up my soul.
O my God, in you I trust; do not let me be put to shame;
    do not let my enemies exult over me.
Do not let those who wait for you be put to shame;
    let them be ashamed who are wantonly treacherous.
Make me to know your ways, O LORD;
    teach me your paths.
Lead me in your truth, and teach me,
    for you are the God of my salvation;
    for you I wait all day long.

—Psalm 25:1-5

REFLECTION

Several years ago, I went through a period of clinical depression. It came on so slowly that I didn't recognize the symptoms. It happened late in the year, in the months of November and December. I remember that year's Advent as a time of struggle—I had no energy; I felt small and vulnerable. I felt unable to participate in any kind of seasonal preparation; I just tried to hang on without going "over the edge." I accompanied friends to a mall to view Christmas decorations, but I couldn't see the colors—only shades of gray. I felt no hope—only gray-colored feelings of despair and grief.

During this time of struggle, I received comfort from those around me. They kept me safe, wrapping me in warm layers of love. They were God's presence to me, giving me hope and filling me with light and life.

Today I remember the gifts of comfort I received during that difficult time, and I look for those who might need God's comfort in their Advent of depression, illness, or grief.

God of comfort, wrap me securely in your nurturing arms. Let me be your voice, your heart, your loving touch to someone who needs a word of grace, a voice of hope, a loving hug during these sometimes difficult Advent days. Amen.

CARRY THESE WORDS IN YOUR HEART TODAY

God waits to comfort me.

Friday

Hope does not build on certainty. To hope means we cannot be completely sure. There are no guarantees. Coming to God with a mixture of hope and excitement is normal and human. We may even experience less welcome feelings alongside hope, such as anxiety, fear, and distrust. But those feelings are acceptable. God welcomes us with whatever degree and quality of hope possible for us. . . . When we anchor our hope in God's steady love and good plans for us, hope becomes a permanent part of us. We have hope not because we are powerful or smart or resourceful but because of who God is. And as we test our hope by acting on it, we release God's power into our circumstances. Our "hope muscle" grows stronger and our desire for God more compelling, just as exercising strengthens our physical muscles. As we consciously work with God, we will see more evidence of God's work in the world around us. The more we hope and watch, the more we will see that reinforces our hope and trust.

—Mary Lou Redding
While We Wait

SCRIPTURE

May the Lord make you increase and abound in love for one another and for all, just as we abound in love for you.

—1 Thessalonians 3:12

REFLECTION

The quote above puts hope in perspective. Hope isn't a simple, sweet sentiment or an unreachable goal. Hope's a bit risky—it's not based on and doesn't rely on some kind of secret-handshake promise from

God. Our hoping does not mean that everything will turn out the way we want it to.

Hope is, instead, a spiritual practice, appropriate any time but especially during the season of Advent. We wait and hope for the coming of Christ into the world. We hope even when it doesn't feel like it's going to make a difference. We hope because we are children of God, children of hope. And the more we hope, the easier it becomes. Our spiritual practice pays off, allowing us to live in hope more and more naturally.

When we hope, we align ourselves more closely with the God of the universe—the eternal force of good, of hope and love and peace.

God of the universe, accept my tentative offerings of hope, and strengthen my practice of hope. Sharpen my vision so that I may see the signs of your goodness at work in the world. I am your partner in hope. Amen.

CARRY THESE WORDS IN YOUR HEART TODAY

I am God's partner in hope.

Saturday

Hope opens something in the human heart. Like shutters slowly parting to admit a winter dawn, hope permits strands of light to make their way to us, even when we still stand in cold darkness; but hope also reveals a landscape beyond us into which we can live and move and have our being. With hope, closely held interior thoughts are gently turned outward; deep desires, perhaps long hidden in secret corners of our heart, might be lifted up to the light. At times, hope peels back the edges of our imagination to free what waits underneath—a changed life, a new resolve, a yes pregnant with possibility. In other moments hope dares us to unfold a layer of desire—for relationship, for clarity, for courage.

—Pamela C. Hawkins
Simply Wait

SCRIPTURE

O LORD, . . .
  we are the clay, and you are our potter;
  we are all the work of your hand.

—Isaiah 64:8

REFLECTION

As we near the end of this first week of Advent, we keep turning toward God, turning toward hope. The Christ child—hope incarnate—is the center of our corporate hope, the trust that this year, in this time and place, we will be transformed by hope. Hope opens closed hearts to love and forgiveness. Hope opens stagnant institutions to new possibilities for justice and restoration. Hope opens the barred doors of hatred and violence and allows new growth in barren war zones.

We, children of God, children of hope, open our lives, relationships, communities, and countries to the transformation that comes from hope. Come, Christ; come, life; come, hope.

God, open our hearts and the heart of the world to your transforming hope. Peel back the layers of our stubborn opinions, our fearful assumptions, and let the light of your life-giving spirit enter in. Amen.

CARRY THESE WORDS IN YOUR HEART TODAY

Hope can open my heart.

Second Week of Advent: Peace

Sunday

While the wolf has yet to live with the lamb and while hurt and destruction continue to plague God's holy mountain, Isaiah's message continues to offer both hope and encouragement. Advent requires not only celebrating the past but also assessing the present and, especially, approaching the future. . . . Isaiah's vision thus need not, and should not, be restricted to that Bethlehem stable; it is a vision that can continue to guide us all.

—Amy-Jill Levine
The Upper Room Disciplines 2004

SCRIPTURE

A shoot shall come out from the stump of Jesse,
     and a branch shall grow out of his roots.
The spirit of the LORD shall rest on him,
     the spirit of wisdom and understanding,
the spirit of counsel and might,
the spirit of knowledge and the fear of the LORD.
. . . .
The wolf shall live with the lamb,
     the leopard shall lie down with the kid,
the calf and the lion and the fatling together,
     and a little child shall lead them.

—Isaiah 11:1-2, 6

REFLECTION

The second candle on the Advent wreath is the candle of peace. When we light the candle of peace, we affirm Isaiah's vision that peace will come on earth. As we move closer to the birth of the Prince of Peace, we are acutely aware of all the places in the world, in our families and relationships, and in our hearts that have not achieved peace. Peace is a vision, a hope, a promise made by the Holy One—that there will be a time when peace will prevail.

Peace, in the global sense, is the cessation of violence between peoples and nations . . . in Israel and Palestine, in Darfur, in Iraq and Afghanistan. We people of peace hold the vision that God's spirit will rest on the leaders of the world and will whisper wisdom in their hearts, wisdom that will guide their actions toward paths of forgiveness, compassion, and peace.

In our own hearts and lives, peace is the calm in the midst of chaos. Each day, may we hold the vision of peace, seeking times of rest and prayer when we open our minds and spirits to God's powerful, gentle peace.

Let peace be our vision.

God of Advent, walk ahead of me, helping me keep sight of your vision of peace. May I hold peace in my heart and pray for peace in our broken world. Amen.

CARRY THESE WORDS IN YOUR HEART TODAY

Let peace begin with me.

Monday

Dear Jesus, during this day help me quiet all the thoughts
that fill my head—where I must go, who I must see, and
what I must do. In their place, give me a sense of your
order, your peace, and your time. . . .

I give all my tasks to you and trust you to bring order
to them.

—Patricia F. Wilson
Quiet Spaces

SCRIPTURE

Blessed be the LORD, the God of Israel,
who alone does wondrous things.

—Psalm 72:18

REFLECTION

Today I echo this prayer from Patricia Wilson, "Jesus, during this day
help me quiet all the thoughts that fill my head." My brain overflows
with anxiety and distractions; I feel as though I might drown under
their pressure.

Surrender is the spiritual discipline I need to practice today.
One by one, I turn over to God each distraction, each crisis, each
fearful thought. I turn over all the feelings and thoughts that sepa-
rate me from the present moment, from other people, from God.

With each surrender I turn my attention in the direction of
God. And with each surrender, the place I have emptied is filled
with a measure of peace.

*God of presence, help me recognize when my thoughts, distrac-
tions, and fears keep me from being fully present to you and to
those around me. I surrender to you all my tasks, my thoughts,*

and my distractions. For you are my peace, and the peace of the world. Amen.

<small>CARRY THESE WORDS IN YOUR HEART TODAY</small>

God, I surrender to you all my cluttered thoughts.

Tuesday

Peacemakers are those who see that the world and its people are broken but also hold a dream, a vision, that God can and does reach out to heal our world. And God does it through the acts of those who live by the values of this new kingdom where God's will is being done.

—Mary Lou Redding
The Power of a Focused Heart

SCRIPTURE

[God] will speak peace to his people,
    to his faithful, to those who turn to [God] in their hearts.
. . . .
Steadfast love and faithfulness will meet;
    righteousness and peace will kiss each other.
Faithfulness will spring up from the ground,
    and righteousness will look down from the sky.
—Psalm 85:8, 10-11

REFLECTION

One of my favorite parts of *Pockets* magazine (The Upper Room's magazine for children) is "Peacemakers at Work." This section of the magazine relates stories of children who are peacemakers. These children have seen God's vision of peace and move toward it through their actions. One child gave up her allowance and raised money for an orphanage in Zimbabwe. Another began at an early age donating her birthday gifts to children in the hospital. A group of Pennsylvania children renovated a barn on their school grounds to create a "Museum of Peace."

These peacemakers inspire me by displaying great faith and vision. They do not hold the cynical view often held by us adults,

"I'm only one person; what can I do?" They understand that no matter how small, their actions in the world today have an impact on the whole.

We can be peacemakers through our hundreds of daily choices: whether to drive a car or walk to the drugstore; to use a washable mug rather than a paper cup; to buy local produce rather than produce grown on another continent and shipped to our location. All of these small choices, small actions, join to make a large impact on the world. With God's guidance we can heal the world.

Loving God, the earth moans, in need of your healing. Help me be a peacemaker today—one who carries your vision and takes the small actions that contribute to healing for the world. Amen.

CARRY THESE WORDS IN YOUR HEART TODAY

God heals the world through me.

Wednesday

Dear Lord, we pray, but it is only by your spirit's power that we can be remade in your likeness. You do it; we cannot even make a start. But you are light, not darkness, and in that knowledge all things are possible. For in the remaking is the peace. In the rebirthing is the life. Only help us keep our eyes on you. Not on the fears, or the limitations, only on your face. The more we see of you, the less we will fear to take on your likeness and lose our own. Amen.

—Hilary McDowell
On the Way to Bethlehem

SCRIPTURE

This is my prayer, that your love may overflow more and more with knowledge and full insight to help you to determine what is best, so that in the day of Christ you may be pure and blameless, having produced the harvest of righteousness that comes through Jesus Christ for the glory and praise of God.

—Philippians 1:9-11

REFLECTION

Being remade in Christ's likeness is our ultimate hope. It's a goal worthy only of God, the creator of the universe: to make us into vessels of love, peace, and compassion.

When shopping, cleaning, planning, or worrying preoccupies us, we forget to leave space for God. When we find ourselves frazzled by chaos, filled with anger or anxiety, we can stop, turn, and look at God. This is the spiritual practice I need these days—keeping my eyes on God.

When, in the midst of my daily tasks and responsibilities, I search for the ways God is present, I am keeping my eyes on God.

When I look for God in each person I meet, in each situation I encounter, I am more open to God's Spirit working in me, shaping me into a vessel of God's peace. Keeping my eyes on God helps me stay open to God's transforming power and allows God to remake me into Christ's likeness. I can then become Christ's heart, mind, and hands in the world.

Creator God, help me keep my eyes on you, that following you, I may be remade into your likeness, a vessel of your love, peace, and compassion. Amen.

CARRY THESE WORDS IN YOUR HEART TODAY

Stop. Turn. Look for God.

Thursday

True lovers of peace are those who, in all their sufferings upon earth, remain at peace in mind and body for the love of Jesus Christ.

—Francis of Assisi
"The Admonitions of Francis" in *The Riches of Simplicity*

SCRIPTURE

A voice cries out:
"In the wilderness prepare the way of the LORD,
    make straight in the desert a highway for our God.
Every valley shall be lifted up,
    and every mountain and hill be made low;
the uneven ground shall become level,
    and the rough places a plain.
Then the glory of the LORD shall be revealed,
    and all people shall see it together,
        for the mouth of the LORD has spoken."

—Isaiah 40:3-5

REFLECTION

Being lovers of peace does not free us from struggle or suffering. Francis of Assisi followed God's calling to minister with the poor despite his wealthy father's protestations. Francis began his ministry by denouncing his family ties, shedding the remnants of that life of privilege (including the clothes he was wearing), and taking a vow of poverty. From that time forward, he traveled the earth barefoot, clad in rough clothing, and living off the charity of others.

True lovers of peace follow God into the wilderness and work to build up God's reign on earth. True lovers of peace shed their expensive garments and live with the outcasts. They put on suits and meet in the halls of power. They teach children in schools and homes and places of worship. True lovers of peace serve in war-torn lands, risking their lives for the ultimate goal of peace. They nurture infants, care for dying loved ones, and offer hospitality to strangers. True lovers of peace search for the face of God in every person they meet.

Let us be true lovers of peace, grounded in the love of Christ, trusting in God's mercy in the midst of suffering.

Ever-loving God, thank you for your presence in difficult situations. Help me be a true lover of peace, at peace in your vast heart. Amen.

CARRY THESE WORDS IN YOUR HEART TODAY

Let me be a true lover of peace.

Friday

Just as we are able to reach out to God with our hearts and minds . . . , we are able to reach out to God with and through our bodies. For it is through our bodies that we see and experience beauty, love, joy, and peace. It is through our bodies that we know the ecstasy of the divine fire burning in our hearts as we enter more deeply into prayer. It is through our bodies that we meet the One who came in a body to dwell among us, heal us, and help us to know God.

—Daniel Wolpert
Creating a Life with God

SCRIPTURE

"By the tender mercy of our God,
    the dawn from on high will break upon us,
to give light to those who sit in darkness
        and in the shadow of death,
to guide our feet into the way of peace."

—Luke 1:78-79

REFLECTION

I want to walk peacefully on the earth, "kissing the Earth with [my] feet," as Thich Nhat Hanh describes it. When I walk gently on the earth or imagine myself kissing the earth with my feet when I walk, I am living in the present moment, aware of my surroundings, conscious of the effect that my walking—or talking or touching—has on those around me and on the web of creation.

Being fully present in my body brings me into this moment—now. Look! I am seeing sunlight (or faces or Christmas lights). Listen! I am hearing music (or angry voices or laughter or silence). Smell! I am in the bakery (or the baby needs changing or the candles are lit).

Taste! I am eating oatmeal (or coffee or something sweet). Feel! I am sitting in a chair (or I am hurting or I am tired).

Being fully present in my body allows me to turn to God more easily, staying open to God's leading in the next moment and the next and the next. I am here, God. What would you have me do? I am here, God. Help me walk in peace. I am here, God. Give me wisdom and strength to face the next challenge.

Walk gently, peacefully, in the way of Christ's peace.

God, I am open and present. Guide my feet into your way of peace. Amen.

CARRY THESE WORDS IN YOUR HEART TODAY

I will walk gently in the way of Christ's peace.

Saturday

The shalom bringers spread a sense of warmth, comfort, hope, and well-being even before a word is spoken. . . .

When we think of these men and women in our lives, we feel as if God is reaching out to us through them. We know that if God is like them—only much more so—then the universe is in safe hands. The glory of God shines through their faces and touches us through their hands.

We call them the children of God.

—Flora Slosson Wuellner
Forgiveness, the Passionate Journey

SCRIPTURE

May the God of steadfastness and encouragement grant you to live in harmony with one another, in accordance with Christ Jesus. . . .

Welcome one another, therefore, just as Christ has welcomed you, for the glory of God.

—Romans 15:5, 7

REFLECTION

The Hebrew word *shalom* means peace. But in its biblical context, it means something more comprehensive than simply the absence of conflict. Shalom means peace, wholeness, healing, safety, rest, the complete goodness that God wishes for us. To be a "shalom bringer" is an honor—someone who pours God's blessings on others, who spreads the good news of life and love and peace.

In this season of preparation, consider ways that you can be a shalom bringer to others. How can you offer signs of God's love to those who need it? How can you bring a sense of safety, wholeness, or healing to ones who feel broken? How can you welcome with love those who feel lonely or estranged?

This Advent, as we pray for peace, let's give thanks to God for the shalom bringers in our lives. What are their names? How have we known God's blessing in our lives through these persons? How might we tell their stories and celebrate the gifts they have given us?

God of wholeness, thank you for the shalom bringers who showed me your glory through the smiles on their faces and the touch of their hands. Help me to be a shalom bringer to one who might need your peace, wholeness, or healing today. Amen.

CARRY THESE WORDS IN YOUR HEART TODAY

Help me be a shalom bringer today.

Third Week of Advent: Joy

Sunday

In joyous anticipation of her firstborn, Mary sings revolution. Enraptured that God chose her, a maiden of no prominence, a woman with no voice, to bear the world's savior, her joy calls up visions of the rich tasting the dust of poverty, the powerful limping with the burden of oppression. . . .

Mary would, I suspect, have us dream dreams and tell tales of hope, the kind of hope that the rich and powerful are too busy and satisfied to entertain, the kind of hope that sustains us in our poverty. That takes knowing our poverty, if not poverty of money, then poverty of intimacy and belonging—the very things our souls need most, the very things that require setting aside possessions and power. Mary's anger frees us to truly celebrate her son's birth. Let her in.

—J. Marshall Jenkins
The Upper Room Disciplines 2006

SCRIPTURE

Mary said,
"My soul magnifies the Lord,
    and my spirit rejoices in God my Savior,
for he has looked with favor on the lowliness of his servant.
    Surely, from now on all generations will call me blessed;
for the Mighty One has done great things for me,
    and holy is his name.
His mercy is for those who fear him
    from generation to generation.

He has shown strength with his arm;
    he has scattered the proud in the thoughts of their hearts.
He has brought down the powerful from their thrones,
    and lifted up the lowly;
he has filled the hungry with good things,
    and sent the rich away empty."

—Luke 1:46-53

REFLECTION

The third candle on the Advent wreath is the candle of joy. In many churches, the third candle is pink (in contrast with purple on weeks one, two, and four) to signify the joy of Jesus' impending birth. The third Sunday of Advent is called Gaudete Sunday. *Gaudete* is Latin for "rejoice." Halfway through the season of preparation, we allow ourselves a little celebration—the Savior is coming, alleluia! We've been waiting, and we must wait a bit longer, but God is coming—soon.

The invitation to rejoice during the season of Advent reminds us to consider the joy that awaits the end of Mary's pregnancy. Mary must have felt joy in carrying a child, in anticipating the birth of her son, the birth of the Savior. Her hymn of praise, the Magnificat, praises God for the great deeds that God has done. The God who proclaims righteousness and justice, who has fed the hungry and sent the rich away, this same God looked on Mary with favor and blessed her with the gift of service to the world.

Our joy calls up visions—what gifts can we expect from the Mighty One who has blessed us and looked upon us with favor?

God of joy, may I dream dreams and share tales of hope as I enter into this third week of Advent. I praise your mighty name. Amen.

CARRY THESE WORDS IN YOUR HEART TODAY
My spirit rejoices in God.

Monday

Joy and peace come into our lives ... when we mind more about God than we do about ourselves, when we realize what the things that matter really are. ...

Joy's very being is lost in the great tide of selfless delight—creation's response to the infinite loving of God. But, of course, the point for us is that this selfless joy has got to go on at times when we ourselves are in the dark, obsessed by the sorrow of life, so that we feel no joy because we cannot gaze at the beauty. Joy is a fruit of the Spirit, not of our gratified emotions. Come, bless the Lord. ... Lift up your hands to the holy place, and bless the Lord.

—Evelyn Underhill
The Soul's Delight

SCRIPTURE

Rejoice always, pray without ceasing, give thanks in all circumstances; for this is the will of God in Christ Jesus for you. Do not quench the Spirit. Do not despise the words of prophets, but test everything; hold fast to what is good; abstain from every form of evil.

—1 Thessalonians 5:16-22

REFLECTION

Sometimes in these days of endless preparation for Christmas, I lose all track of joy. I bustle to finish up work at the office, so I can take time off to be with loved ones. I attend parties and try to squeeze in a shopping trip on the way home. Then I find myself sitting frustrated in miles of traffic. I've lost the joy, and I'm pretty much left alone with myself—tired, grumpy, and fed up. I might even say to myself, *It would be easier not to have Christmas. It's just too much work.*

In times like these, joy becomes an action rather than a feeling. Joy's presence in the world doesn't depend on our feelings.

Joy surrounds; we simply open our eyes and heart to God's presence. Remember God. Remember God's presence and gifts. Rejoice in God's action in the world.

In this busy season, we can pray for drivers in front of and behind us in a traffic jam. We can give thanks for friendships, food, and fellowship at a party. We can think of ways God works through us in the workplace. We can notice signs of God's joy—the beauty of colors, the diversity of people, the warmth of the sun, the miracle of birth. We can take an action of joy.

God, when I am joyless, help me stop, turn to you, and take actions of joy. Let me join with you in selfless joy. Amen.

CARRY THESE WORDS IN YOUR HEART TODAY

I will open my eyes to see God's joy.

Tuesday

It is God's will that we have true delight with God in our salvation and that we be mightily comforted and strengthened. And so God wants our souls to be occupied joyfully with God's grace. For we are God's bliss, for God delights in us without end, and so, by God's grace, will we delight in God.

—Julian of Norwich
Encounter with God's Love

SCRIPTURE

Surely God is my salvation;
   I will trust, and will not be afraid,
for the LORD GOD is my strength and my might;
   he has become my salvation.
With joy you will draw water from the wells of salvation.

—Isaiah 12:2-3

REFLECTION

"We are God's bliss, for God delights in us without end, and so, . . . will we delight in God." Julian of Norwich wrote these words during the dark days of the Middle Ages when the Black Death was sweeping through England (1348–50), wiping out 30-40 percent of the population. Julian, an anchoress, mystic, and author, wrote a book in which she described visions of Christ speaking with her.

Julian's understanding of God was unusual for her day and time. Rather than believing in a vengeful God, she wrote of a divine being who delights in humankind and invites us to delight in God in return. Julian's ideas are radical even today. How often do we consider ourselves to be "God's bliss" or accept the notion that God delights in us? Usually, we keep a running tally of our actions that displease God.

But our joyful, generous, grace-filled God sends Christ to the world in the form of a baby, a baby we can hold, a baby who assures us of God's love and nurture while affirming God's desire for love and nurture from us.

God of delight, let me see the world today through your joyful eyes. Let me feel your love for me and neighbor; may I join with you in delighting in all that you have created. Amen.

CARRY THESE WORDS IN YOUR HEART TODAY

God delights in me; I delight in God.

Wednesday

Thank you, God, that even when I feel empty and dry, I know that the springs of joy are there, buried deep within me. I ask you to tap those springs now, release them, and carry me away on their fullness.

Thank you, O God, for joy.
 Joy that overcomes all else.
   Joy that is more powerful than the darkest powers.
     Joy that is more abundant than the waters in the seas.
       Joy that is mine.

—Patricia F. Wilson
Quiet Spaces

SCRIPTURE

When the LORD restored the fortunes of Zion,
   we were like those who dream.
Then our mouth was filled with laughter,
   and our tongue with shouts of joy;
then it was said among the nations,
   "The LORD has done great things for them."
The LORD has done great things for us,
   and we rejoiced.

Restore our fortunes, O LORD,
   like the watercourses in the Negeb.
May those who sow in tears reap with shouts of joy.
Those who go out weeping,
   bearing the seed for sowing,
shall come home with shouts of joy, carrying their sheaves.

—Psalm 126

A good friend's husband was diagnosed with a life-threatening illness. Together they went through two months of unknowns, hospitalization, and surgeries. Later, she reflected on that time and said, "Not once during those months was I afraid. I was so grateful for all the people who were helping in so many ways. And I found that I could not be grateful and fearful at the same time."

Gratitude and its close cousin, joy, result from action, not just feeling. Active joyfulness brings with it an awareness of who we are and an acknowledgment that all we have are gifts from a generous, loving God. We search for signs of the good in the people and situations around us. We work to give up selfish perspectives and join more closely in the movements of God in the world.

Living from the perspective of gratitude and joy, our hearts remain open to the Spirit's influence; we stay connected to God's guidance. Being grateful for God's good in our lives displaces our fears and dissatisfactions and replaces them with God's presence.

Loving God, help me be the face of joy to someone who might be struggling today. If I am facing struggles of my own, gently guide my thoughts toward gratitude, that I may rejoice always in you. Amen.

CARRY THESE WORDS IN YOUR HEART TODAY

Replace my fear with gratitude.

Thursday

Allowing ourselves to mourn develops our capacity to feel life's joys. I believe that positive and negative emotions are two sides of the same coin. Of course, many of us would prefer to experience and deal with only positive feelings. We often feel uncomfortable with our own or others' sadness, anger, disappointments, fears. . . . As we learn to feel all our feelings, we explore what it means to be fully human, to be all that God created us to be.

—Mary Lou Redding
The Power of a Focused Heart

SCRIPTURE

The spirit of the Lord GOD is upon me,
    because the LORD has anointed me;
he has sent me to bring good news to the oppressed,
    to bind up the brokenhearted,
to proclaim liberty to the captives,
    and release to the prisoners;
to proclaim the year of the LORD's favor,
    and the day of vengeance of our God;
    to comfort all who mourn.

—Isaiah 61:1-2

REFLECTION

It's hard to be in a place of sadness during Advent and Christmas. The culture proclaims cheerfulness and happiness. Others expect us to participate in the joy of the season and feel uncomfortable with brokenheartedness and grieving.

But our sadness and mourning, especially in the midst of Advent and Christmas, positions us right where we are supposed to be—in the present moment, feeling whatever feelings reside within us right now. Even in the instance of long-ago loss, we naturally bring to mind the sadness of remembering, the mourning of lost loved ones, lost hopes or dreams at this time of year.

There is room for all at the manger. The good news of Christ's birth comes to the oppressed, bent over by grief; the brokenhearted, full of tears; those imprisoned by depression and despair. Christ comes to comfort all who mourn, trusting that in God's time joy will replace sadness.

God of the brokenhearted, it is hard to be in mourning during this joyous time of year. But I know that you come to all of us, especially those filled with tears as captives to grief. Wrap them in your comforting spirit. Amen.

CARRY THESE WORDS IN YOUR HEART TODAY
God comforts all who mourn.

Friday

The most audacious, enlivening, freeing, joy-creating, humbling, and life-transforming reality of the Christian faith is not that God will be with us, but that God is here, right now. God is here in the midst of suffering, in the midst of joy, in the midst of shortcoming, in the midst of triumph, in the midst of our greatest fulfillment, and in the midst of our brokenheartedness.

—Gregory S. Clapper
When the World Breaks Your Heart

SCRIPTURE

When John heard in prison what the Messiah was doing, he sent word by his disciples and said to him, "Are you the one who is to come, or are we to wait for another?" Jesus answered them, "Go and tell John what you hear and see: the blind receive their sight, the lame walk, the lepers are cleansed, the deaf hear, the dead are raised, and the poor have good news brought to them."

—Matthew 11:2-5

REFLECTION

Many years ago, I went through a "dark night of the soul," a crisis of faith. I felt deeply disappointed by my family and other significant people in my life. Wounded and vulnerable, I questioned God. I was angry at God, disappointed that I had not been saved from deep wounding. I felt that I no longer knew anything for sure about God. My beliefs were stripped away, one by one, until all that was left was a simple knowledge that God existed. I did not know who God was or what God was doing, but I knew God *was*.

In the midst of my turmoil, I held on to my belief that *God Is*. That simple knowledge kept me from coming apart in the crisis.

And over time, my faith and God's presence renewed themselves within me.

When I look back on that time, I see that God was with me throughout. It was *my* crisis, not God's. God gently held me through my questioning and my struggle. God never let go but kept me wrapped in love, sheltering me from my own self-destruction. God was with me; God never left.

When I have lost my way, God is. When I am found again, God is. When all around me is chaos, God is. When all around me is peace, God is. When I face tragedy, God is. When I face triumph, God is. Thank you, God. Amen.

CARRY THESE WORDS IN YOUR HEART TODAY

God is here, right now.

Saturday

O God whose mercy is upon generation after generation, fill my spirit with the joy of your Spirit! Grant me the gift of joyous expectation, seeing your coming in a million ways and responding with blessing, with leaping, and with joy. Amen.

—Marjorie Hewitt Suchocki
The Upper Room Disciplines 2000

SCRIPTURE

Sing aloud, O daughter Zion; shout, O Israel!
Rejoice and exult with all your heart, O daughter Jerusalem!
The LORD has taken away the judgments against you,
    he has turned away your enemies.
The king of Israel, the LORD, is in your midst;
    you shall fear disaster no more.
On that day it shall be said to Jerusalem: Do not fear, O Zion;
    do not let your hands grow weak.
The LORD, your God, is in your midst, a warrior who gives victory;
he will rejoice over you with gladness,
    he will renew you in his love;
he will exult over you with loud singing as on a day of festival.

—Zephaniah 3:14-18

REFLECTION

We end this third week of Advent with a spirit of joyous expectation. Soon the Christ child's birth will fulfill our hopes and dreams. As we look toward Christ's arrival, we watch for signs, "seeing [God's] coming in a million ways and responding with blessing, with leaping, and with joy!"

We see signs of Christ's coming in the concluding of Advent preparation. We are completing tasks and finishing projects. As we finish these stages of preparation, we open up space and time in our lives and our hearts. We may have more time to rest and reflect on the closing days of Advent, more time for prayer, more time for joy, more time to sit with friends and loved ones.

We see signs of Christ's coming in the rising excitement of children; in the yearning words of the Advent hymns; in the expectant, growing love we feel in our hearts. We see signs of Christ's coming when we recognize Jesus' face in the harried mother at the store, in the homeless folks who spend a warm night within the safety of the church, in the generous donations of strangers to the Salvation Army ringer.

> *God of Advent joy, keep my eyes and heart open to signs of your coming. May I be joyously expectant, seeing your coming in a million ways. Amen.*

CARRY THESE WORDS IN YOUR HEART TODAY
I will keep my eyes and heart open to signs of God's coming.

Fourth Week of Advent: Love

Sunday

There is one task only: the task of love. We are called by God to live this life with love for everyone. All that we do can be an expression of God's love. However mundane the task, perform it with a generous spirit and grateful heart. The most insignificant task performed with love is tribute to God.

—Christopher Maricle
The Jesus Priorities: 8 Essential Habits

SCRIPTURE

Now the birth of Jesus the Messiah took place in this way. When his mother Mary had been engaged to Joseph, but before they lived together, she was found to be with child from the Holy Spirit. Her husband Joseph, being a righteous man and unwilling to expose her to public disgrace, planned to dismiss her quietly. But just when he had resolved to do this, an angel of the Lord appeared to him in a dream and said, "Joseph, son of David, do not be afraid to take Mary as your wife, for the child conceived in her is from the Holy Spirit. She will bear a son, and you are to name him Jesus, for he will save his people from their sins." . . . When Joseph awoke from sleep, he did as the angel of the Lord commanded him; he took her as his wife, but had no marital relations with her until she had borne a son; and he named him Jesus.

—Matthew 1:18-21, 24-25

REFLECTION

The fourth candle on the Advent wreath is the candle of love. That seems so appropriate in this last week of Advent, the final days before we receive God's greatest gift to us—divine Love wrapped in swaddling clothes, lying in a manger.

Joseph's place in this drama is one of love. Engaged to Mary, he discovers that she is pregnant. Even the visit of an angel probably does not answer all of his questions or calm all of his fears. But Joseph, I like to think, acts out of love. Love and trust make up for any doubts he might have about his role in this matter. Joseph takes Mary as his wife and makes room in his heart for her son, whom he names Jesus.

We certainly don't play such a dramatic role as Joseph in God's story, but we are, nevertheless, important to the whole. Every action we take, every small or large task we perform, is woven in love into God's cosmic story.

God of love, may everything I do become an expression of your love. Amen.

CARRY THESE WORDS IN YOUR HEART TODAY

Each task performed with love is a tribute to God.

Monday

Love is had only by loving. If you want love, you must begin by loving—I mean you must want to love. Once you want it, you must open the eye of your understanding to see where and how love is to be found. And you will find it within your very self.

—Catherine of Siena
A Life of Total Prayer

SCRIPTURE

In the sixth month the angel Gabriel was sent by God to a town in Galilee called Nazareth, to a virgin engaged to a man whose name was Joseph, of the house of David. The virgin's name was Mary. And he came to her and said, "Greetings, favored one! The Lord is with you." But she was much perplexed by his words and pondered what sort of greeting this might be. The angel said to her, "Do not be afraid, Mary, for you have found favor with God. And now, you will conceive in your womb and bear a son, and you will name him Jesus. He will be great, and will be called the Son of the Most High, and the Lord God will give to him the throne of his ancestor David."

—Luke 1:26-32

REFLECTION

God's great love for the world is manifest in God's gift of Jesus to us. Into a world filled with fear, uncertainty, and discord, God sends hope, saying, "I am with you." Into a world ruled by human wants and greed, God sends love, saying, "I will show you the way." God begins by loving the people of the world, choosing Mary to be love incarnate to the baby Jesus.

God sent the angel Gabriel to tell Mary she was going to have a baby. Her initial reaction sounds like one of healthy fear. But

God's message stated, "Do not be afraid." God anticipated Mary's human reactions of fear and mistrust and sent the message of assurance: "You can trust me and my intention for love in the world." Mary's trust in God and her ability to set aside her fears made her a nurturing vessel for God's love to be born into the world.

Fear and mistrust sometimes block my ability to love others. If I am not centered or rooted in God, I tend to react to every new or unusual situation from a stance of fear. Fear takes over and keeps me from seeing God's presence in the situation. If I begin with fear, fear is what I will receive.

Catherine of Siena says, "If you want love, you must begin by loving." When I can put aside my fear and turn those fears over to God, I become more able to give and receive love. Today may I be a nurturing vessel for God's love in the world.

God, help me set aside my fear and my mistrust so that I can begin each interaction, each situation, in love. Amen.

CARRY THESE WORDS IN YOUR HEART TODAY

I begin by loving.

Tuesday

Love is the capacity to see both the good and evil in people but to love the good; to see both the excellent and mediocre but to encourage the excellent; to see the wellness and the sickness and to strengthen the wellness. Before all else, love is the capacity to see everyone and everything as interconnected, "held together" in one cosmic embrace.

—Robert Corin Morris
Provocative Grace

SCRIPTURE

O LORD God of hosts,
   how long will you be angry with your people's prayers?
You have fed them with the bread of tears,
   and given them tears to drink in full measure.
You make us the scorn of our neighbors;
   our enemies laugh among themselves.

Restore us, O God of hosts;
   let your face shine, that we may be saved.
   . . . .
But let your hand be upon the one at your right hand,
   the one whom you made strong for yourself.
Then we will never turn back from you;
   give us life, and we will call on your name.

Restore us, O LORD God of hosts;
   let your face shine, that we may be saved.

—Psalm 80:4-7, 17-19

REFLECTION

In these last few days before Christmas, our world seems to shrink. We become part of a universal yearning for peace, for goodness, for love. The world views each natural disaster through hearts of compassion. Each house fire or car accident or cancer patient slipping away is felt through hearts of love. All of us yearn for the signing of peace agreements and the laying down of weapons by warring sides.

Evil, sickness, and human apathy don't disappear during these days. But our common humanity binds us together in God's "cosmic embrace." We are one body, at least for a few days. We feel one another's pain and bear together injustice and scorn. We cry tears for one another, embracing with love both friend and stranger. We see the good in others, setting aside our quick judgments and sharp tongues. God bathes our world with love, and we respond in love with healing and compassion.

God, today may I love the good I see, encourage the excellence
I encounter, and strengthen the wellness in need of nurture. For
you hold us all together in a warm, cosmic embrace. Amen.

CARRY THESE WORDS IN YOUR HEART TODAY

Love sees the good in others.

Wednesday

Why is it so hard for us to believe that God's love really is unconditional and that we should imitate God's love not only for others but also for ourselves?

Perhaps we have regarded self-centered behavior too harshly. We are unwilling or unable to give ourselves the same gentle grace that God offers us and that we believe should be offered to others. Leap from doubt to belief and remember that God loves you, delights in you, and yearns for your response.

—Rueben P. Job
A Guide to Prayer for All Who Seek God

SCRIPTURE

When Elizabeth heard Mary's greeting, the child leaped in her womb. And Elizabeth was filled with the Holy Spirit and exclaimed with a loud cry, "Blessed are you among women, and blessed is the fruit of your womb. And why has this happened to me, that the mother of my Lord comes to me? For as soon as I heard the sound of your greeting, the child in my womb leaped for joy. And blessed is she who believed that there would be a fulfillment of what was spoken to her by the Lord."

—Luke 1:41-45

REFLECTION

The God of Elizabeth and Mary, of Joseph and Jesus, is a God of abundant love, grace, and blessing. This generous God chose Elizabeth (old and barren) and Mary (young and unmarried) to be the mothers of John the Baptist and Jesus the Christ. This creative God doesn't follow convention. This God is full of surprises, joy, and extravagant grace.

Excitement and joy fill the union of Mary and Elizabeth in today's scripture reading. Elizabeth reports to Mary, "As soon as I heard the sound of your greeting, the child in my womb leaped for joy." The unusual journeys of these cousins join together in God's story. Elizabeth continues, "Blessed is she who believed that there would be a fulfillment of what was spoken to her by the Lord." I can imagine God's delight in this meeting of those chosen women.

The God of this story loves us in the same way today—abundantly, unconditionally, with delight and an occasional surprise. God offers me the same gentle grace and love that I see in the story of Elizabeth and Mary. This God expects me to open my heart to that God-delight and to share that unconditional love with myself and others.

Thank you, God, for your delight in me. Let me move from doubt to belief, trusting in your extravagant grace. Let me be your love, grace, and delight for others today. Amen.

CARRY THESE WORDS IN YOUR HEART TODAY

I can trust God's extravagant love.

Thursday

The important thing is not to think much but to love much; and so do that which best stirs you to love.

—Teresa of Avila
The Soul's Passion for God

SCRIPTURE

But you, O Bethlehem of Ephrathah,
    who are one of the little clans of Judah,
from you shall come forth for me one who is to rule in Israel,
whose origin is from of old, from ancient days.
Therefore he shall give them up until the time
    when she who is in labor has brought forth;
then the rest of his kindred shall return to the people of Israel.
And he shall stand and feed his flock in the strength of the LORD,
    in the majesty of the name of the LORD his God.
And they shall live secure, for now he shall be great
    to the ends of the earth;
and he shall be the one of peace.

—Micah 5:2-5

REFLECTION

Teresa of Avila lived in a Carmelite convent in the 1500s. While I have never lived in a formal community such as a convent or a monastery, I have lived with others and know that love can be difficult to show to those with whom one lives.

In these final days before Christmas, feelings run high and patience runs low. I can easily let my anxiety or busyness keep me from paying attention to what matters most. I become short with family members and expect perfection from all around me. I focus on what's wrong rather than what's right and become critical and unforgiving. I might even be downright unpleasant to be around!

Today I will try Saint Teresa's advice not to "think much but to love much." I will let go of all that is not essential, knowing that as long as I am rooted in love, all shall be well. Seen through eyes and hearts of love, today is blessed.

God of love, help me put aside my critical, compulsive thinking and search for the way of love. Amen.

CARRY THESE WORDS IN YOUR HEART TODAY

Think less; love more.

Friday

God calls us to come home for Christmas. God calls us to come back from all those places where we have settled for less than the fullness of life promised to us in Christ. God calls us back from all the ambitions and possessions we have pursued, thinking they would satisfy us. God calls us to let go of any bitterness and resistance to forgive that block the light of love from warming us. . . . God calls us to come home and to rest, to be embraced by one who loves us as we are. God offers us a place where we are fully known and also fully accepted.

—Mary Lou Redding
While We Wait

SCRIPTURE

I will appoint a place for my people Israel and will plant them, so that they may live in their own place, and be disturbed no more; and evildoers shall afflict them no more, as formerly, from the time that I appointed judges over my people Israel; and I will give you rest from all your enemies. Moreover the LORD declares to you that the LORD will make you a house.

—2 Samuel 7:10-11

REFLECTION

"God calls us to come home for Christmas," Mary Lou Redding writes. For some, the concept of going home for Christmas may not bring comfort. But whether our childhood home offered refuge or not, all of us long for a place to call our own. A place where we will be "disturbed no more," where "evildoers shall afflict [us] no more," where we will have "rest from all [our] enemies." Second Samuel declares the good news that God will "make you a house." It is this home to which God calls us this Christmas.

In this home with God, we can let down our guard; we can rest in love; we can let go of all the things we have not done or we have not done correctly. We can open our hearts to God's comfort and healing and let go of those things that block God's grace from enfolding us.

We open up our minds, hearts, and arms for God's embrace. God has opened wide the doors of God's home. Let us come in.

God of love, I long to come home to you this day. Help me lay aside all my baggage and enter through your open doors. Let me rest in your love and grace. Amen.

CARRY THESE WORDS IN YOUR HEART TODAY

God is calling me home to rest in the embrace of love.

Christmas and Epiphany: Presence

Christmas Eve

O Holy Night,
that deepening darkness above and around,
light-pierced and silence-shrouded,
out of which little children are called in
and seeking shepherds are sent out.
O night of nights,
you spread across heaven
and touch the earth,
surrounding God's people,
capturing us in a moment of holy time,
like a globe protects a precious flicker of Light.
Come,
draw us in,
hold us together
while we wait for the birth of the Light of lights,
the One who will guide us into the world anew. Amen.

—Pamela C. Hawkins
Simply Wait

SCRIPTURE

In that region there were shepherds living in the fields, keeping watch over their flock by night. Then an angel of the Lord stood before them, and the glory of the Lord shone around them, and they were terrified. But the angel said to them, "Do not be afraid; for see—I am bringing you good news of great joy for all the people: to you is born this day in the city of David a Savior, who is the Messiah, the Lord. This will be a sign for you: you will find a child wrapped in bands of cloth and lying in a manger." And suddenly there was with the angel a multitude of the heavenly host, praising God and saying,

"Glory to God in the highest heaven,
and on earth peace among those whom he favors!"

—Luke 2:8-14

REFLECTION

Our days of work and waiting are over; we have arrived at Christmas Eve. This holy day invites us to sit in breathless anticipation of the event for which we have prepared these last few weeks. In a few hours, the "Light of lights" will enter the darkened world, bathing each face, each heart, each darkened corner with the light of God's love.

In this final day of preparation, take some time to be quiet and sweep out any remaining debris from the corners of your heart. Ask God to knock down any remaining barriers to God's fullness and presence in your life. Quiet your mind and your spirit so that it will be ready for the gift that is coming.

Take a few minutes during the day to reflect on these past days of Advent. Remember the places and people through which you have encountered God's presence. Make a list of the things you are grateful for today. Consciously give to God those things that hinder you from accepting God's delight in you. End your reflection time with silence or prayer.

Light of lights, I sit in comfortable darkness, knowing that you will soon arrive. Make me ready to receive your blessings and share the good news of your arrival. Come soon, Holy One. Amen.

CARRY THESE WORDS IN YOUR HEART TODAY
May I receive God's blessings.

Christmas Day

Gentle, loving God,
You come to me this day
in the form of a tiny, vulnerable baby.
I look on you with wonder and gratitude.
Glory to you in the highest heaven,
For it is in the name of your child, Jesus,
that we pray.
Amen.

—Beth A. Richardson
Child of the Light

SCRIPTURE

Make a joyful noise to the LORD, all the earth;
    break forth into joyous song and sing praises.
Sing praises to the LORD with the lyre,
    with the lyre and the sound of melody.
With trumpets and the sound of the horn
    make a joyful noise before the King, the LORD.

Let the sea roar, and all that fills it;
    the world and those who live in it.
Let the floods clap their hands;
    let the hills sing together for joy
at the presence of the LORD.

—Psalm 98:4-9

REFLECTION

Our God is love. Whether we find ourselves surrounded by family
and friends or alone in a quiet house, our God is love. Whether we
are in familiar surroundings or in a foreign land, our God is love.

Whether we are living in abundant health or weighed down by a failing body, our God is love.

Our God is love: inside us, outside us, clothing us, immersing us, comforting us, girding us, feeding us, holding us—in love.

God of love, I am yours. May I rest in your love today, in joy and thanksgiving. Amen.

Rejoice. My God is love.

December 26

Let Christ be born in you!
Let hope be born, Let love be born.
Let newness of heart be born in you!
Let gentleness be born, Let truth be born.
Let concern for the poor be born in you!
Let generosity be born, Let compassion be born.
Let close communion with God be born in you!
Let prayer be born, Let action be born.
Let the faith to take up your cross and follow be born in you!
And let it lead you in the ways of our Lord,
For the sake of our Lord. Now and always.
Amen.

—Alive Now

SCRIPTURE

In the beginning was the Word, and the Word was with God, and
the Word was God. He was in the beginning with God. All things
came into being through him, and without him not one thing came
into being. What has come into being in him was life, and the life
was the light of all people.

—John 1:1-4

REFLECTION

Christ's presence has entered the joyous and wounded world . . .
and has entered our lives too. What does it mean for Christ to be
born in us today? Christ-born-in-us brings promises of new life in
the spirit: healing of wounds, love despite suspicion or hatred, compassion instead of impatience, joy where there is sadness.

Christ born in the world brings promises of faith that turn
into action: gentleness and truth born in our leaders, compassion
and justice for the poor and the oppressed.

What needs to be born or born anew in us today?

Creating God, all things came into being through you. Bring new life into being inside of me, that I may better reflect your hope, your love, and your grace to those around me. Let Christ be born in me today. Amen.

CARRY THESE WORDS IN YOUR HEART TODAY

Let Christ be born in me.

December 27

Consider for a moment what, in practice, the word *adoration* implies. The upward and outward look of humble and joyful admiration. Awestruck delight in the splendor and beauty of God, the action of God and Being of God, in and for God's self alone, as the very color of life: giving its quality of unearthly beauty to the harshest, most disconcerting forms and the dreariest stretches of experience. This is adoration: not a difficult religious exercise, but an attitude of the soul.

—Evelyn Underhill
The Soul's Delight

SCRIPTURE

I will greatly rejoice in the LORD,
    my whole being shall exult in my God;
for he has clothed me with the garments of salvation,
    he has covered me with the robe of righteousness,
as a bridegroom decks himself with a garland,
    and as a bride adorns herself with her jewels.
For as the earth brings forth its shoots,
    and as a garden causes what is sown in it to spring up,
so the Lord GOD will cause righteousness and praise
    to spring up before all the nations.

—Isaiah 61:10-11

REFLECTION

This time of year we sing, "O come, let us adore him, Christ the Lord." I like Evelyn Underhill's description of the meaning of adoration—"Awestruck delight in the splendor and beauty of God, . . . not a difficult religious exercise, but an attitude of the soul."

These twelve days after Christmas make up the liturgical season of Christmastide. Unlike retailers, we Christians are still in the midst of Christmas celebration. There are no markdowns on Christmas love, no sweeping off the shelves of Christmas joy. Our hearts fill with adoration, and our eyes search for evidence of the splendor and beauty of God.

As we stand next to the manger, let us look on Christ with adoration and gratitude, praising God with our whole beings.

God of splendor, let me be awestruck today by the beauty of your works. May I come before you with adoration and humble gratitude. Amen.

CARRY THESE WORDS IN YOUR HEART TODAY

May I be awestruck by God's splendor and beauty.

December 28

In our crowded and distracted days, one of the ancient paths to deepening communion with God is attentiveness. . . . This vital attentiveness is nourished . . . by love. It is reflected in the attention a young mother and father lavish upon their newborn infant, the finely honed appreciation shared by longtime friends, the alert care of an adult child at the bedside of a frail parent. Love pierces the fog of suspended animation that often surrounds us, and brings us to greater consciousness of God's presence in what we are seeing and hearing.

—John S. Mogabgab
Weavings

SCRIPTURE

Now after [the wise ones] had left, an angel of the Lord appeared to Joseph in a dream and said, "Get up, take the child and his mother, and flee to Egypt, and remain there until I tell you; for Herod is about to search for the child, to destroy him." Then Joseph got up, took the child and his mother by night, and went to Egypt, and remained there until the death of Herod.

—Matthew 2:13-15

REFLECTION

On this day the church has traditionally observed "The Feast of the Holy Innocents" when it remembers the children Herod slaughtered in his attempt to kill the Christ child sought by the Magi. (Read the whole story in Matthew 2.) Even the powerful story of Jesus' birth does not escape the sorrow of death and destruction. Joseph's attentiveness to God's voice alerted him to the danger and allowed Joseph to guide Mary and Jesus to safety in Egypt.

In these days of intense distraction, I find it difficult to give my attention to any one thing. Multitasking, doing several things at once, without paying attention to any one thing, seems to be the norm. However, when I am unable or unwilling to stop and give my attention to a single task, all the tasks suffer. A phone conversation with a friend is diminished when I am also checking my e-mail. A work task is done halfway when I attempt several chores at the same time. And my connection with God suffers if I'm meditating as I rush out the door on my way to work. What I value deserves my full attention.

God's love nourishes our attentiveness. When we are surrounded by distractions, fear, or grief, God's love pierces our fogs and brings us closer to peace.

Loving God, I offer to you today every thought, feeling, or situation that keeps me separated from you. Send your love to disperse my fog and bring me closer to you. Amen.

CARRY THESE WORDS IN YOUR HEART TODAY

Love clears the fog that separates me from God.

December 29

At some moment in the day, deliberately gaze at a tree, a shrub, a flower, a bird, a cloud, sunlight, rain, and greet it as a loving partner. Look at it fully and lovingly. Touch it if you can or open your palms to its presence. Let God's love speak, reach out to you through it. Move gently deeper than the outward appearance and greet the hidden, living mystery.

—Flora Slosson Wuellner
Prayer, Stress, and Our Inner Wounds

SCRIPTURE

Praise the LORD from the earth,
    you sea monsters and all deeps, fire and hail, snow and frost,
stormy wind fulfilling his command!

Mountains and all hills, fruit trees and all cedars!
Wild animals and all cattle, creeping things and flying birds!

Kings of the earth and all peoples,
    princes and all rulers of the earth!
Young men and women alike,
    old and young together!

Let them praise the name of the LORD,
    for his name alone is exalted;
    his glory is above earth and heaven.
He has raised up a horn for his people,
    praise for all his faithful,
    for the people of Israel who are close to him.
Praise the LORD!

—Psalm 148:7-14

REFLECTION

God speaks to me through creation. Throughout the year I watch God's creation from my breakfast table. During the winter months, the birds visit my bird feeder and birdbath. The birds "neither sow nor reap nor gather into barns" (Matt. 6:26), yet they trust and do not worry. In the spring, I watch each day as pear trees, then redbuds, then dogwoods, open their beautiful blossoms. The neighborhood becomes transformed into a fairyland with the vivid colors of new life. In late summer, mushrooms begin to grow in my yard. A thumb-sized nub grows quickly over a couple of days. A little tube unfurls its roof and soon it's a full-sized mushroom that then disappears back into the earth. In the early fall, I watch the spiders weave their intricate webs, delicate but strong enough to capture their food. Their patience to build, to wait, and to rebuild leaves me in awe.

Take some time today to notice the beauty of God's earth and to join its living mystery.

Creating God, you created the birds, the mushrooms, the sea monsters of the deep—and you created me. Open my eyes, my ears, and my senses today that I may become one with your living mystery. Amen.

CARRY THESE WORDS IN YOUR HEART TODAY
I will greet the hidden, living mystery in today.

December 30

God comes to the woman who feels in exile in her own marriage, for the man who grieves the loss of life dreams. God comes to the child who lives on the street, for the parents who struggle to feed and clothe their children. God comes to the one whose loneliness or depression intensifies every Christmas. . . .

. . . Emmanuel—God-with-Us—is coming to us, to meet us wherever we are—happy or sad, joyous or grieving. God comes to stand with us, whatever our condition. And we thank God for that promised gift of presence.

—Beth A. Richardson
Child of the Light

SCRIPTURE

It was fitting that God, for whom and through whom all things exist, in bringing many children to glory, should make the pioneer of their salvation perfect through sufferings. For the one who sanctifies and those who are sanctified all have one Father. For this reason Jesus is not ashamed to call them brothers and sisters, saying,
"I will proclaim your name to my brothers and sisters,
  in the midst of the congregation I will praise you."
And again,
"I will put my trust in him."
And again,
"Here am I and the children whom God has given me."

—Hebrews 2:10-13

REFLECTION

As I listen to the news or read the paper today, I realize that many people are suffering. Their suffering reminds me that soon after this

Christmas and Epiphany observance, Christians will enter the church season of Lent and Holy Week and follow Jesus' road to crucifixion and death. Even as we celebrate Jesus' birth, we know the challenges that are coming.

Because we are human, we experience happiness and sorrow, joy and suffering, times of welcoming new life and mourning life's passing. God's child, Jesus, experienced human life just as we do. And we have, as he did, the gift of God's presence with us in everything we face. Whatever we encounter, God is with us.

Ever-present God, thank you for your gift of standing-with-us. In happiness, in grief, in loving, or in pain, you are our constant companion. You are with us. We are not alone. Amen.

CARRY THESE WORDS IN YOUR HEART TODAY

God is with me wherever I am.

December 31—New Year's Eve

God is beyond but also near, transcendent and immanent. Seen not only with telescopic vision but also in the microscopic view of deep intimacy. God is the Source beyond my imagining and also the Love who is immediately present. God, the Center of all, dwells at the center of my being. So when I am centered, I open the eyes of my heart to perceive God's presence, transcendent in glory and present here and now. I receive the gift of an intimate relationship with God deeper than words can express. I let go of my efforts to reach God and simply rest in the love of the Trinity. I let go of my attachments and surrender myself to Christ. I release whatever thoughts come to me and consent to the Presence and to the restoring action of the Spirit within.

—J. David Muyskens
Forty Days to a Closer Walk with God

SCRIPTURE

O LORD, our Sovereign,
   how majestic is your name in all the earth!

You have set your glory above the heavens.
   Out of the mouths of babes and infants
you have founded a bulwark because of your foes,
   to silence the enemy and the avenger.

When I look at your heavens, the work of your fingers,
   the moon and the stars that you have established;
what are human beings that you are mindful of them,
   mortals that you care for them?

Yet you have made them a little lower than God,
   and crowned them with glory and honor.

You have given them dominion over the works of your hands;
  you have put all things under their feet,
all sheep and oxen,
  and also the beasts of the field,
the birds of the air, and the fish of the sea,
  whatever passes along the paths of the seas.

O LORD, our Sovereign, how majestic is your name in all the earth!

—Psalm 8

REFLECTION

On this eve of a new year, I think of the world as seen in those photographs from outer space—a blue and green sphere resting in a sea of blackness. This image helps me gain perspective—I am not at the center. Even our earth is not at the center. The center is beyond me, beyond us. Only God can hold the center around which all creation revolves.

As you come to the close of a year, take some time—thirty minutes to an hour—to reflect on the past year. What things made you happy? What accomplishments were you proud of and want to remember by recording in a journal or on a list? What situations or relationships make you uncomfortable to remember? Write down your responses and note any action you need to take. Close with silence or a short time of prayer, offering the past year to God.

God of all, guide me as I journey into a new year. Celebrate with me the progress I have made in becoming a person of love. Give me strength to right any wrongs, to keep growing into the person you would have me to be. Guide me into this new year, filled with hope, optimism, compassion, and love. Amen.

CARRY THESE WORDS IN YOUR HEART TODAY

God dwells at the center of all.

January 1—New Year's Day

Loving God, journey with me this year
so that I may feel your presence,
abide in your forgiveness, grow in your strength,
and dwell in your love.
Give me an open heart,
an open mind,
and open eyes
so that I may sing your praise
and follow your path always and everywhere. Amen.

—Larry James Peacock
Openings

SCRIPTURE

For everything there is a season, and a time for every matter under heaven:
a time to be born, and a time to die;
a time to plant, and a time to pluck up what is planted;
a time to kill, and a time to heal;
a time to break down, and a time to build up;
a time to weep, and a time to laugh;
a time to mourn, and a time to dance;
a time to throw away stones, and a time to gather stones together;
a time to embrace, and a time to refrain from embracing;
a time to seek, and a time to lose;
a time to keep, and a time to throw away;
a time to tear, and a time to sew;
a time to keep silence, and a time to speak;
a time to love, and a time to hate;
a time for war, and a time for peace.

—Ecclesiastes 3:1-8

REFLECTION

Today we start a new year. Turning to a new calendar, our lives resound with possibility. What joys will this new year bring to our families and friends, to our world? As we dedicate our lives and this coming year to God, we take time to connect with God and offer our lives to God's service.

Today set aside thirty minutes to an hour to reflect on the coming year. What are your hopes and dreams for life, family, community, or world? What things within yourself, at the job, or among relationships need work or improvement? What places need healing or reconciliation? Record your responses, and note any action that you need to take. Close with silence or a short time of prayer, offering the coming year to God.

God of new beginnings, guide me through the seasons of the coming year. Whatever joy or hardship I face, let me face it standing with you. Whatever building up or tearing down that I encounter, let me take action under your care. For you are the creator of every season. Amen.

CARRY THESE WORDS IN YOUR HEART TODAY

Loving God, journey with me this year.

January 2

God, let us count the ways you never leave us. Your Light of Day greeted us this morning. The smell of life filled our nostrils with the crisp, chilly air of a new day. The melody of gently crackling leaves whispered your love in our ears. These are among the Good Morning gifts we thank you for. You have given us another day in your Precious Presence.

Come what may this day: angry traffic, angry words, paved roads, paved ways, we will praise your Holy Name! And so we greet you this day with shouts of joy and thanksgiving. Amen.

—Sherrie Dobbs Johnson
The Africana Worship Book

SCRIPTURE

I will recount the gracious deeds of the LORD,
    the praiseworthy acts of the LORD,
because of all that the LORD has done for us,
    and the great favor to the house of Israel
that he has shown them according to his mercy,
    according to the abundance of his steadfast love.
For he said, "Surely they are my people,
    children who will not deal falsely";
and he became their savior in all their distress.
It was no messenger or angel but his presence that saved them;
in his love and in his pity he redeemed them;
    he lifted them up and carried them all the days of old.

—Isaiah 63:7-9

REFLECTION

The gift of God's presence sustains us today. It feels like a long time since Christmas. The new year has begun, and we haven't heard

Christmas music on the radio in over a week. People around us seem to have forgotten their holiday generosity; folks have already resumed old habits.

But God is still with us, blessing us with signs of presence and love. We are alive today; thank you, God. We are blessed with the things we need to live a full life; thank you, God. And we are walking side by side with God, who showers us with steadfast love.

As we play Christmas music today in our home, car, or office, we remember the joy and gratitude of Christmas Day. We give thanks for the many gifts of the past few weeks. Our gratitude generates action: a call to a lonely friend, an e-mail of thanks to the church staff, a personal psalm of praise in our journal.

Thank you, God, for your gift of presence that sustains me today. If I am too weak or broken, lift me up and carry me as you did in the days of old. Amen.

CARRY THESE WORDS IN YOUR HEART TODAY

God lifts me up and carries me.

January 3

Sometimes I think we make Jesus too small. Jesus is not small. Jesus is big. Yes, he was a little baby born in Bethlehem, but he's more than that! He was a preacher and a healer, but he's more than that. He was the Savior nailed to the cross whispering forgiveness to the world, but he's more than that. He is the one risen from the grave; the conqueror over sin, death, and evil; but he's even more than that. In the magnificent words of Paul, he is the image of the invisible God, the one through whom all things were made and in whom everything holds together (Col. 1:15-17). When we are overwhelmed by this vision of Jesus, our response can only be, "Jesus, you are the one I want to love and follow."

—Trevor Hudson and Stephen D. Bryant
The Way of Transforming Discipleship

SCRIPTURE

When the fullness of time had come, God sent his Son, born of a woman, born under the law, in order to redeem those who were under the law, so that we might receive adoption as children. And because you are children, God has sent the Spirit of his Son into our hearts, crying, "Abba! Father!" So you are no longer a slave but a child, and if a child then also an heir, through God.

—Galatians 4:4-7

REFLECTION

In the face of the mystery of Jesus, both human and divine, I respond with the authors of today's quote, "Jesus, you are the one I want to love and follow." The little baby in the manger—I can understand that. But healer, preacher, teacher, Savior, Son of God, conqueror of death—added all up, these go beyond my ability to comprehend.

I want to do the right thing. I yearn to follow the path that leads to life. How many times a day should I pray? What's the right combination of spiritual disciplines? Which devotional should I read? How many times a week should I attend corporate worship? And how do I know when I've got the right combination down?

Jesus said, "Follow me." It's that simple. Let go, follow my heart, and affirm, "Jesus, you are the one I want to love and follow."

Jesus, keep prodding me to follow you, and all else will fall into place. Amen.

CARRY THESE WORDS IN YOUR HEART TODAY

Jesus, you are the one I want to love and follow.

January 4

Physicists today are pointing out that our sun is one of millions of suns in our galaxy and our galaxy is one of more than 150 billion-plus galaxies. . . . And when I think about that, my mouth gapes open in awe.

Yet God's greatness is not the most awesome discovery. The most awesome is what we learn from revelation—that the God of 150 billion galaxies cares about me, about you, grains of sand on an endless seashore. That, you see, is what the whole of revelation tells us, that God, the God of this vast universe, loves us with an infinite love. "While we were still sinners, Christ died for us. That proves God's love," the Apostle Paul put it (Rom. 5:8, author's translation).

—E. Glenn Hinson
Spiritual Preparation for Christian Leadership

SCRIPTURE

Praise the LORD!
Praise the LORD from the heavens;
   praise him in the heights!
Praise him, all his angels; praise him, all his host!

Praise him, sun and moon; praise him, all you shining stars!
Praise him, you highest heavens, and you waters above the heavens!

Let them praise the name of the LORD,
   for he commanded and they were created.

—Psalm 148:1-5

REFLECTION

I often lose perspective on things. I tend to think that everything is about *me*. I'm the center of the universe; everything, everyone, revolves around me. It's a shock when I discover (over and over again) that it's not about me. I'm just a tiny grain of sand "on an endless seashore." Talk about feeling small. . . .

Hinson's quotation of scientific fact puts my universe into perspective—the universe *definitely does not* revolve around us. It puts human existence into perspective—we are one part of God's gigantic creation. And yet, we are loved and cared for by God as unique individuals, God's special children in whom God delights.

Today, when things are not going *my* way, I will remember the image of 150 billion galaxies—with God at their center.

> *Creative and creating God, thank you for creating the universe with its vast galaxies. And thank you for creating me, infinitely tiny in comparison but precious in your sight. Amen.*

CARRY THESE WORDS IN YOUR HEART TODAY

The God of 150 billion galaxies cares about me.

January 5

Slowly but surely we can cultivate the habits of mind and heart that put us in touch with the "mind of Christ," that is, the spirit in which he dealt with the rough edges of human experience. Our lives, like his, are meant to be carried along in the steady flow of the Spirit of God. And surely, for Jesus, practicing the presence of God keeps him available to that flow.

—Robert Corin Morris
Wrestling with Grace

SCRIPTURE

As God's chosen ones, holy and beloved, clothe yourselves with compassion, kindness, humility, meekness, and patience. Bear with one another and, if anyone has a complaint against another, forgive each other; just as the Lord has forgiven you, so you also must forgive. Above all, clothe yourselves with love, which binds everything together in perfect harmony. And let the peace of Christ rule in your hearts, to which indeed you were called in the one body. And be thankful. Let the word of Christ dwell in you richly.

—Colossians 3:12-16

REFLECTION

If I could adopt and nurture one spiritual practice this year, it would be learning to let myself be "carried along in the steady flow of the Spirit of God." This means setting aside my opinions, my control, my will, my need to be right, and placing myself in God's care, asking God to be in charge of everything I think and say and do.

If I'm in tune with God's presence, I imagine that being carried along in the flow of God's Spirit is a gentle process. But if I'm struggling to be in charge, it's liable to be a turbulent ride, perhaps a bit like running the rapids of a river in a rubber dinghy. I'm learning that if I live inside of God's care and will, a bumpy ride is not God's fault but some resistance in me.

If I can learn to relax and let God be in charge, I can grow in this spiritual practice. It is not always easy. Every day brings challenges. But I can make choices that keep my own spirit open to the presence of God's Spirit—and enter into the steady flow of the heart and mind of Christ.

> *Great God of life, your Spirit flows around me and over me every moment. Help me open myself to your presence, that I may join with you and be carried along in the steady flow of your Spirit. Amen.*

CARRY THESE WORDS IN YOUR HEART TODAY

Carry me in the steady flow of your Spirit.

January 6—Epiphany

Ever-loving God, who came into the world clothed in our garment of flesh and who willingly gave yourself to the cross, clothe us in your own Spirit, that persons will recognize you in us and receive your great gift of love. In the name of Jesus, your greatest gift. Amen.

—Norman Shawchuck and Rueben P. Job
A Guide to Prayer for All God's People

SCRIPTURE

Arise, shine; for your light has come,
　　and the glory of the LORD has risen upon you.
For darkness shall cover the earth, and thick darkness the peoples;
but the LORD will arise upon you, and his glory will appear over you.
Nations shall come to your light,
　　and kings to the brightness of your dawn.

Lift up your eyes and look around;
　　they all gather together, they come to you;
your sons shall come from far away,
　　and your daughters shall be carried on their nurses' arms.
Then you shall see and be radiant; your heart shall thrill and rejoice,
because the abundance of the sea shall be brought to you,
　　the wealth of the nations shall come to you.
A multitude of camels shall cover you,
　　the young camels of Midian and Ephah;
　　all those from Sheba shall come.
They shall bring gold and frankincense,
　　and shall proclaim the praise of the LORD.

—Isaiah 60:1-6

REFLECTION

Today we, along with the wise ones, arrive at Epiphany. We have been on a long journey together, and finally we have reached the end. We arrive at the birthplace of joy, and we kneel in gratitude at the scene before us. When we look around with the eyes of our hearts, we see generations of those who have come before, from all nations and ages, from all races and cultures. All have arrived at this simple manger to give thanks for the great gift of Love.

As we arise from our place at the side of the Christ child, we go forth into the world, recipients of abundant grace, bathed in love, and clothed in God's Spirit. We are ready to journey forward into the glow of Epiphany light, spreading the good news of God's great gift to the world. Come along. Walk with us as we follow Christ's light.

Ever-loving God, thank you for the gift of this pilgrimage of faith through the days of Advent and Christmas. Send me out into your world surrounded by Epiphany light, that I may be your mind, heart, and hands in the world. Amen.

CARRY THESE WORDS IN YOUR HEART TODAY

Let me be Christ's hands, heart, and spirit in the world.

Group Study Guide

ADVENT IS A CHALLENGING SEASON during which to carve out time for study, reflection, and prayer. For that very reason, it's the right time to schedule a short-term Sunday school class or Wednesday night group.

This group study guide is designed for use during the four weeks of Advent, one hour per week. The purpose for meeting together during Advent is to

1. Deepen and broaden the personal experience of using this book during Advent.

2. Develop additional avenues for support during this stressful time of year.

3. Take time with God in a corporate setting.

4. Assist individuals in going deeper with themes from each week of Advent.

FOR THE LEADER

As leader you help to create a safe and intentional place for group members to travel through this Advent/Christmas season, reflecting on the ways that God is at work in their individual lives. Before each session, read over the outline for that week's group time. Be sure to gather any extra supplies or resources needed to lead the group.

Order the books several weeks in advance and make sure each participant has a book. If your group sessions are not on Sunday, think about whether the first group gathering might occur during the week preceding the first Sunday of Advent.

At the first session, lead the participants in developing some common guidelines that will make the group a safe place for the Advent and Christmas journey. You may start with the guidelines on the next page but invite the group members to add their own suggestions.

Group Guidelines

THIS GROUP WILL ENCOURAGE and provide mutual support for individual journeys through the Advent and Christmas seasons. Participants agree to meet weekly during four weeks of Advent and come prepared to the group sessions. The leader will assure that the group will start and end on time. Participants agree as follows:

- To be present at every session. If unable to attend, alert the leader so group members can continue to support you in your absence.

- Respect what other people say. Share from your own experience. Don't give advice or try to fix another person. Honor another person's experience by listening deeply and not focusing your mind on what you will say next.

- Give others time to share. Be sensitive to the amount of time you speak, and make sure that others have time also. At the same time, know that sharing in the group is not mandatory. If someone does not wish to say anything, please respect that person's desire.

- Observe confidentiality. What others talk about in the group stays in the group.

- Don't fear the silence. If no one has anything to say, rest in the quiet. God can speak through the silence.

Participants may want to exchange phone numbers or e-mail addresses to be in touch with one another for support during the coming weeks.

First Week of Advent: Hope

Materials: Hymnals, Advent wreath and candles, lighter or matches, paper, pencils or pens, newsprint or whiteboard and markers.

GATHERING/CENTERING

Sing together, read responsively, or listen to an Advent hymn such as "O Come, O Come, Emmanuel." Light the first candle of the Advent wreath.

Say: **Today we light the first candle on the Advent wreath. This candle of hope reminds us that we place our hope in God and the gift God gives us in Jesus. The light from this candle reminds us that God is with us in this time together. Thanks be to God. Amen.**

Take care of any housekeeping details before continuing. Make sure everyone has a book, talk about group guidelines, and encourage persons who use e-mail or text messages to sign up for the daily reminders sent by text or e-mail (unclutteredheart.org). If group members are new to having daily reflection time, invite more experienced members to share what has worked for them.

REFLECT

Lead the group through a discussion of the following questions. If the number of participants is too large (more than six or so) for meaningful group discussion, form smaller groups so all may have a chance to speak.

- What have been your experiences of trying to remember God during previous Advent seasons?

- What sorts of daily meditations or reflection times have worked for you?

- Take a moment to think about your intention for this Advent and Christmas season—the goals you have set for yourself and your journey with God. (Examples: Read the book each morning, and write in my journal. Sign up for a daily text message or e-mail and take time out for prayer when the message arrives. Get an Advent buddy to check in with a couple of times a week by phone or by e-mail.) Those who feel comfortable may share their goals with the group.

GOING DEEPER

This week you will lead a "Hope Workout." Begin by brainstorming as a group what people are hoping for. Record the hopes on newsprint or whiteboard. Ask: **What are you hoping for this week? for the Advent season? for Christmas? for the coming year?**

After brainstorming, say: **In this week's reading Mary Lou Redding mentions the fact that when we hope, we exercise our "hope muscle." The action of hoping makes it easier to hope. What energy shifts did you sense within yourself or within the group as we talked about our hopes?**

Invite people into a time of silence (5-10 minutes) to consider the questions below. Provide paper and pencils for people to make notes. Say: **Consider the following questions. Make some notes to yourself if that would be helpful. Where is hope most needed for yourself? for your community? for the world?**

At the end of the silent time, invite participants to turn to one or two other people to share their hopes.

CLOSING

Ask participants to speak aloud any prayer concerns or particular hopes they would like the group to know about. Is anyone facing particular challenges in the coming week?

Join in the following litany:

Leader: O God, we are hoping for . . . (a *participant speaks aloud a hope*).

All respond: **God, you are our hope.**

(Continue in this fashion until all hopes have been shared or you feel a need to end the litany.)

Close with this prayer:

> **O God, thank you for being our hope. Carry us into this week upheld by powerful hope. Let us be your beacons of hope for people and places weighed down by hopelessness. As we enter together with you into this Advent journey, help us to be your mind, heart, and hands in the world. For we pray in your name. Amen.**

Second Week of Advent: Peace

Materials: Hymnals, Advent wreath and candles, lighter or matches, paper, pencils or pens.

GATHERING/CENTERING

Sing together, read responsively, or listen to an Advent hymn, such as "Come, Thou Long-Expected Jesus." Light the first two candles of the Advent wreath.

Say: **Today we light the first two candles on the Advent wreath. The first candle is the candle of hope. As we light the second candle, the candle of peace, we remember that the Prince of Peace is coming. We are called, with him, to be peacemakers in a broken world. God is with us in our time together. Thanks be to God. Amen.**

REFLECT

Lead the group through a discussion of the following questions. If the number of participants is too large (more than six or so) for meaningful group discussion, form smaller groups so all may have a chance to speak.

- How have you seen, heard, or experienced God working in your life or in the world today? In the past week?

- What have been your experiences in trying to remember God during your busy days?

- When you think of the Advent theme of peace, what comes to your mind? Brainstorm the places in your life, your community, and the world that need peace.

- What are the desires of your heart as we enter into a week with the theme of peace?

GOING DEEPER

This week's activity helps participants create a breath prayer that will help them find peace in the coming week.

Say: Our Going Deeper activity today involves an exercise that will help you develop a breath prayer. It is a prayer that articulates your deepest needs in the form of words spoken silently while you are breathing.

Ask people to be quiet and to get into a comfortable position. Guide them slowly through the process of composing a breath prayer by reading each of the following steps twice and by giving participants time to think and pray before moving to the next step.

Think of the name of God that is most meaningful to you. Repeat this name over and over again in your mind. (Repeat the instructions.)

Answer these questions: What is my heart's desire? What is my dream? What do I long for? (Repeat.)

Using your name for God, create a brief prayer that lifts to God your deepest desire. The breath prayer should be only six or eight syllables—for example, "Comforter, take away my pain." (Repeat.)

Now repeat your prayer silently, over and over as you breathe. As you inhale, say your name for God. As you exhale, speak your prayer.

After 1–2 minutes, bring the activity to a close. Invite participants to write down their breath prayer. Let them know that they may change their breath prayer at any time. If they encounter a difficult situation or uncomfortable feelings, they can create the breath prayer that speaks to them at that moment.

Adapted from page 17 of the **devozine** *Guide for Mentors and Small Groups* 9, no. 6 (November/December 2006). Copyright © 2006 by Upper Room Ministries.

CLOSING

Ask participants if they have any prayer concerns they would like to share or if they are facing particular challenges in the coming week before closing with a time of prayer.

Third Week of Advent: Joy

Materials: Hymnals, Advent wreath and candles, lighter or matches, Bible, paper, pencils or pens.

GATHERING/CENTERING

Sing together, read responsively, or listen to an Advent hymn such as "My Soul Gives Glory to My God" or "Hail to the Lord's Anointed." Light the first three candles of the Advent wreath.

Say: **Today we light the first three candles on the Advent wreath. The first candle is the candle of hope. The second candle is the candle of peace. As we light the third candle, the candle of joy, we remember the joy of Mary. With Mary, we praise God for the wonderful deeds of God in the world. We affirm that God is with us in our time together. Thanks be to God. Amen.**

REFLECT

Lead the group through a discussion of the following questions. If the number of participants is too large (more than six or so) for meaningful group discussion, form smaller groups so all may have a chance to speak.

- How have you seen, heard, or experienced God working in your life or in the world today? In the past week?

- What have been your experiences in trying to remember God during your busy days?

- What blocks you from experiencing joy in your life? in the life of your community? in the world?

- What are the desires of your heart as we enter a week with the theme of joy?

GOING DEEPER

Say: This week's Going Deeper activity focuses on the experience of Mary as recorded in Luke 1.

Invite participants to close their eyes, to be still, to breathe deeply, and to be aware of God's presence. Ask them to imagine the scene described in Luke 1:26–38 as you read aloud the passage.

Then say: **Rewind and replay this scene in your mind. Pause the scene when you want to look and listen more closely.** (Allow a few minutes of silence.)

Now rewind again to a particular part of the scene that captured your attention. Listen to what is said. Imagine what is felt. Look for God's presence. (Allow a few minutes of silence.)

Imagine that you are Mary and that the angel has come to you. Hear God's call as if it were directed to you. (Allow a few minutes of silence.)

These are Mary's words. Repeat them quietly after me. (Read aloud Luke 1:46–55, pausing to allow people to repeat each phrase. Allow another minute of silence.)

Take a moment to give thanks and praise to God.

When you are ready, open your eyes.

Invite participants to write their thoughts and feelings about this experience. Then ask them to form groups of three and to interview one another about the exercise. Explain that one person is to ask questions, another is to answer, and the third is to listen without speaking. Encourage the people in each group to switch roles until everyone has had a chance to be interviewed.

- What about your experience was similar? different?
- What insights did you gain from one another?
- What aspect of Mary's experience touches you most deeply? Why?

CLOSING*

Ask members to stand in a circle. Read aloud the phrases below, and invite people, after each one, to look at one another and respond, "and you."

God chooses you . . .

> and you.

God claims you . . .

> and you.

God calls you . . .

> and you

and names you . . .

> and you.

God surprises you . . .

> and you.

God comes to you . . .

> and you

and makes a home with you . . .

> and you.

God is born in you . . .

> and you.

God grows in you . . .

> and you.

God raises you . . .

> and you

and blesses you . . .

> and you.

God sees you . . .

    and you.

God is pleased with you . . .

    and you.

Ask: Knowing that God's life has been poured into us to grow within us, to become visible to others, and to transform the world, how will our lives be changed?

Invite the group to offer prayers of praise and commitment.

*Adapted from page 17 of the **devozine** *Guide for Mentors and Small Groups* 7, no. 6 (November/December 2004). Copyright © 2004 by Upper Room Ministries.

Fourth Week of Advent: Love

Materials: Hymnals, Advent wreath, lighter or matches, paper, glue, scissors, magazines, newspapers, pens or pencils, whiteboard or newsprint and markers.

GATHERING/CENTERING

Sing together, read responsively, or listen to an Advent hymn such as "Lo, How a Rose E'er Blooming." Light all four candles of the Advent wreath.

Say: Today we light all four candles on the Advent wreath. The first candle is the candle of hope. The second candle is the candle of peace. The third candle is the candle of joy. This fourth candle is the candle of love. God sent love to us in the form of a baby: Jesus, the Christ. We wait in love for Christ's coming. God is with us now in our time together. Thanks be to God. Amen.

REFLECT

Lead the group through a discussion of the following questions. If the number of participants is too large (more than six or so) for meaningful group discussion, form smaller groups so all may have a chance to speak.

- How have you seen, heard, or experienced God working in your life or in the world today? In the past week?

- What have been your experiences in trying to remember God during your busy days?

- When you think of the Advent theme of love, what comes to your mind? Brainstorm the places—both in your life, your community, and the world—in need of love.

- What barriers keep you from loving others? from loving God?

- What are the desires of your heart as we follow love into this final week of Advent?

GOING DEEPER

This week's Going Deeper invites participants to focus on love and the things that encourage or block their ability to create places of love in their lives, communities, or world. Participants will consider the reflection questions and create a collage, drawing, or list to illustrate what they need to create an environment of love.

Say: **Let us move into a time of silence during which I invite you to create a collage, a drawing, or a list of what you require to create a loving environment. What is it that you need to create the most loving experience for you, for your friends and family? Paper and pencils/pens, magazines, newspapers, scissors, and glue—these things are available for you to create this in a visual way. Use the following questions to inspire your creation.**

Questions
(list these questions on whiteboard or newsprint)

- What does your heart require for love to have the best chance to be present and nurtured?
- What do you need in your home environment to create a loving experience?
- What is required to create love in your church? community? corporate setting? world?

Allow ten or fifteen minutes for participants to create their pieces. Then invite them to share their work in groups of two or three.

CLOSING

Ask participants if they have any prayer concerns they would like to share.

Pray this litany together.

Leader: O God, we need your love in so many places. We raise before you these people, places, or situations that need your love . . . (*participants name aloud a person, place, or situation in need of God's love*).

As a need is named, all respond: God, send your love.

(Continue in this fashion until all hopes have been shared, or you feel a need to end the litany.) Close with this prayer:

God of love, we await your coming with eager antici-pation. In this final week before Christmas, may every-thing we do become an expression of your love. We thank you for the privilege of this Advent journey together. Bless all of us here here, our family and friends, as we enter this season of love. We pray in Christ's name. Amen.

Advent and Christmas Litanies

USE THESE LITANIES during the corporate worship time at your church or during your family devotional time during Advent and Christmas. These litanies are based on the scriptures from the Revised Common Lectionary, Year C.

Permission is granted to use these litanies in corporate worship. If prayers are reproduced, please add the following credit line: From *The Uncluttered Heart* by Beth A. Richardson. Copyright © 2009 by Upper Room Books. Used by permission.

FIRST WEEK OF ADVENT: HOPE

Keep awake. Stay alert. The kingdom of God is near.

> *We are God's partners in hope.*

The days are surely coming when God will fulfill the promise.

> *We are God's partners in hope.*

A righteous branch will spring up and will bring forth justice.

> *We are God's partners in hope.*

Stand up. Raise your hands. Your redemption is drawing near.

> *We are God's partners in hope.*

As we light this first Advent candle, the candle of hope, may we be partners in hope, witnesses to the promise that hope is coming—it is being born into the world. Amen.

—Based on Jeremiah 33:14-16 and Luke 21:25-36

SECOND WEEK OF ADVENT: PEACE

The voice of one crying out in the wilderness: "Prepare the way of the Lord, make his paths straight."

> *Walk gently in the way of peace.*

"Every valley shall be filled, and every mountain and hill shall be made low."

Walk gently in the way of peace.

"The crooked shall be made straight, and the rough ways made smooth."

Walk gently in the way of peace.

"All flesh shall see the salvation of God."

Walk gently in the way of peace.

We light the first Advent candle and remember that hope is coming. As we light the second Advent candle, the candle of peace, we remember that the Prince of Peace is coming, and we join in the work of preparing the way. We walk gently in the way of peace. Amen.

—Based on Luke 3:1-6 and Isaiah 40:3-5

THIRD WEEK OF ADVENT: JOY

Surely God is our salvation; we will trust and will not be afraid.

With joyous expectation we watch for signs of God's coming.

God is our strength and our might. With joy we will draw water from the wells of salvation.

With joyous expectation we watch for signs of God's coming.

Give thanks to God, call on God's name; make known God's deeds among the nations.

With joyous expectation we watch for signs of God's coming.

Shout aloud and sing for joy, for great in our midst is the Holy One.

With joyous expectation we watch for signs of God's coming.

We light the first two Advent candles, the candle of hope and the candle of peace. As we light the third candle, the candle of joy, we join the heavens and the earth in praising God's holy name. With joyous expectation, we watch for signs of God's coming. Amen.

—Based on Isaiah 12:2-6

FOURTH WEEK OF ADVENT: LOVE

Our souls magnify the Lord, and our spirits rejoice in God.

We trust in God's extravagant love.

The Mighty One has done great things. Holy is God's name.

We trust in God's extravagant love.

Mercy is for those who fear God from generation to generation.

We trust in God's extravagant love.

God has brought the powerful from their thrones, and lifted up the lowly. God has filled the hungry with good things and sent the rich away empty.

We trust in God's extravagant love.

We light the first three Advent candles, the candles of hope, peace, and joy. As we light the fourth candle, the candle of love, we open our hearts to God's love. It waits to fill our hearts that we may be signs of God's extravagant love for the whole world. Amen.

—Based on Luke 1:46-55

CHRISTMAS EVE OR DAY

How beautiful upon the mountains are the feet of the messenger who announces peace, who brings good news, who announces salvation, who says to Zion, "Your God reigns."

Let Christ be born in us.

Listen! Your sentinels lift up their voices; together they sing for joy, for in plain sight they see the return of the Lord.

Let Christ be born in us.

Break forth together into singing, you ruins of Jerusalem; for the Lord has comforted the people and has redeemed Jerusalem.

Let Christ be born in us.

All the ends of the earth shall see the salvation of our God.

Let Christ be born in us.

As we light the Christ candle, we welcome the tiny babe, born in a manger. Hope of the world, bringer of peace, joy of our hearts, and love incarnate, we welcome you. Let Christ be born in us today. Amen.

—Based on Isaiah 52:7-10

Notes

From page 20 of *A Guide to Prayer for All Who Seek God* by Norman Shaw-chuck and Rueben P. Job. Copyright © 2003 by Norman Shawchuck and Rueben P. Job. All rights reserved. Used by permission of Upper Room Books.

INTRODUCTION

Saint Theophan the Recluse in *The Art of Prayer: An Orthodox Anthology*, comp. Igumen Chariton of Valamo, trans. E Kadloubovsky and E. M. Palmer, ed. Timothy Ware (London: Faber and Faber, 1966), 119.

M. Basil Pennington, "A Christian Way to Transformation," *Spirituality Today*, 35, no. 3 (Fall 1983), 220–29.

Week One

SUNDAY

From page 368 of *Openings: A Daybook of Saints, Psalms, and Prayer* by Larry James Peacock. Copyright © 2003 by Larry James Peacock. All rights reserved. Used by permission of Upper Room Books.

MONDAY

From "God's Song, Our Song" by Heather Murray Elkins, from page 360 of *The Upper Room Disciplines 2006: A Book of Daily Devotions*. Copyright © 2005 by Upper Room Books. All rights reserved. Used by permission of Upper Room Books.

TUESDAY

From page 18 of *Leading a Life with God: The Practice of Spiritual Leadership* by Daniel Wolpert. Copyright © 2006 by Daniel Wolpert. All rights reserved. Used by permission of Upper Room Books.

WEDNESDAY

From pages 369–370 of *A Guide to Prayer for All Who Seek God*, by Norman Shawchuck and Rueben P. Job. Copyright © 2003 by Norman Shawchuck and Rueben P. Job. All rights reserved. Used by permission of Upper Room Books.

THURSDAY

From page 20 of *Setting the Christmas Stage: Readings for the Advent Season* by John Indermark. Copyright © 2001 by John Indermark. All rights reserved. Used by permission of Upper Room Books.

FRIDAY

From pages 23–24 of *While We Wait: Living the Questions of Advent* by Mary Lou Redding. Copyright © 2002 by Mary Lou Redding. All rights reserved. Used by permission of Upper Room Books.

SATURDAY

From pages 43–44 of *Simply Wait: Cultivating Stillness in the Season of Advent* by Pamela C. Hawkins. Copyright © 2007 by the author. All rights reserved. Used by permission of Upper Room Books.

Week Two

SUNDAY

From "The God of All" by Amy-Jill Levine, page 347 in *The Upper Room Disciplines 2004: A Book of Daily Devotions*. Copyright © 2003 The Upper Room. All rights reserved. Used by permission of Upper Room Books.

MONDAY

From page 89 of *Quiet Spaces: Prayer Interludes for Women* by Patricia F. Wilson. Copyright © 2002 by Patricia F. Wilson. All rights reserved. Used by permission of Upper Room Books.

TUESDAY

From page 93 of *The Power of a Focused Heart: Eight Life Lessons from the Beatitudes* by Mary Lou Redding. Copyright © 2006 by Mary Lou Redding. All rights reserved. Used by permission of Upper Room Books.

WEDNESDAY

From page 151 of *On the Way to Bethlehem: Reflections on Christmas for Every Day in Advent* by Hilary McDowell. Copyright © 2000 by Hilary McDowell. All rights reserved. Used by permission of Upper Room Books.

THURSDAY

From page 40 of *The Riches of Simplicity: Selected Writings of Francis and Clare*, edited by Keith Beasley-Topliffe. Copyright © 1998 by Upper Room Books. All rights reserved. Used by permission of Upper Room Books.

FRIDAY

From pages 116–117 of *Creating a Life with God: The Call of Ancient Prayer Practices* by Daniel Wolpert. Copyright © 2003 by Daniel Wolpert. All rights reserved. Used by permission of Upper Room Books.

SATURDAY

From page 123 of *Forgiveness, the Passionate Journey: Nine Steps of Forgiving Through Jesus' Beatitudes* by Flora Slosson Wuellner. Copyright © 2001 by Flora Slosson Wuellner. All rights reserved. Used by permission of Upper Room Books.

Week Three

SUNDAY

From "Celebrating with Mary" by J. Marshall Jenkins, page 365 of *The Upper Room Disciplines 2006: A Book of Daily Devotions*. Copyright © 2005 by Upper Room Books. All rights reserved. Used by permission of Upper Room Books.

MONDAY

From pages 31–32 of *The Soul's Delight: Selected Writings of Evelyn Underhill*, edited by Keith Beasley-Topliffe. Copyright © 1998 by Upper Room Books. All rights reserved. Used by permission of Upper Room Books.

TUESDAY

From page 29 of *Encounter with God's Love: Selected Writings of Julian of Norwich*, edited by Keith Beasley-Topliffe. Copyright © 1998 by Upper Room Books. All rights reserved. Used by permission of Upper Room Books.

WEDNESDAY

From page 44 of *Quiet Spaces: Prayer Interludes for Women* by Patricia F. Wilson. Copyright © 2002 by Patricia F. Wilson. All rights reserved. Used by permission of Upper Room Books.

THURSDAY

From page 31 of *The Power of a Focused Heart: Eight Life Lessons from the Beatitudes* by Mary Lou Redding. Copyright © 2006 by Mary Lou Redding. All rights reserved. Used by permission of Upper Room Books.

FRIDAY

From page 105 of *When the World Breaks Your Heart: Spiritual Ways of Living with Tragedy*, by Gregory S. Clapper. Copyright © 1999 by Gregory S. Clapper. All rights reserved. Used by permission of Upper Room Books.

SATURDAY

From "A Holy Waiting," by Marjorie Hewitt Suchocki, page 371 of *The Upper Room Disciplines 2000: A Book of Daily Devotions*. Copyright © 1999 by Upper Room Books. All rights reserved. Used by permission of Upper Room Books.

Week Four

SUNDAY

From page 93 of *The Jesus Priorities: Eight Essential Habits* by Christopher Maricle. Copyright © 2007 by Christopher Maricle. All rights reserved. Used by permission of Upper Room Books.

MONDAY

From page 13 of *A Life of Total Prayer: Selected Writings of Catherine of Siena*, edited by Keith Beasley-Topliffe. Copyright © 2000 by Upper Room Books. All rights reserved. Used by permission of Upper Room Books.

TUESDAY

From page 31 of *Provocative Grace: The Challenge in Jesus' Words* by Robert Corin Morris, Copyright © 2006 by Robert Corin Morris. All rights reserved. Used by permission of Upper Room Books.

WEDNESDAY

From pages 389–90 of *A Guide to Prayer for All Who Seek God* by Norman Shawchuck and Rueben P. Job. Copyright © 2003 by Norman Shawchuck and Rueben P. Job. All rights reserved. Used by permission of Upper Room Books.

THURSDAY

From pages 58–59 of *The Soul's Passion for God: Selected Writings of Teresa of Avila*, edited by Keith Beasley-Topliffe. Copyright © 1997 by Upper Room Books. All rights reserved. Used by permission of Upper Room Books.

FRIDAY

From page 45 of *While We Wait: Living the Questions of Advent* by Mary Lou Redding. Copyright © 2002 by Mary Lou Redding. All rights reserved. Used by permission of Upper Room Books.

CHRISTMAS EVE

From page 104 of *Simply Wait: Cultivating Stillness in the Season of Advent* by Pamela C. Hawkins. Copyright © 2007 by Pamela C. Hawkins. All rights reserved. Used by permission of Upper Room Books.

CHRISTMAS DAY

From page 84 of *Child of the Light: Walking through Advent and Christmas* by Beth A. Richardson. Copyright © 2005 by Beth A. Richardson. All rights reserved. Used by permission of Upper Room Books.

DECEMBER 26

From *Alive Now* Web page, November/December 2003, copyright © 2003 by The Upper Room.

DECEMBER 27

From page 20 of *The Soul's Delight: Selected Writings of Evelyn Underhill*, edited by Keith Beasley-Topliffe. Copyright © 1998 by Upper Room Books. All rights reserved. Used by permission of Upper Room Books.

DECEMBER 28

From "Editor's Introduction" of *Weavings: A Journal of the Christian Spiritual Life* 17, no. 4 (July/August 2002.) Copyright © 2002 by Upper Room Ministries. All rights reserved.

DECEMBER 29

From page 73 of *Prayer, Stress, and Our Inner Wounds* by Flora Slosson Wuellner. Copyright © 1985 by The Upper Room. All rights reserved. Used by permission of Upper Room Books.

DECEMBER 30

From page 58 of *Child of the Light: Walking through Advent and Christmas* by Beth A. Richardson. Copyright © 2005 by Beth A. Richardson. All rights reserved. Used by permission of Upper Room Books.

New Year's Eve—December 31

From pages 13–14 of *Forty Days to a Closer Walk with God: The Practice of Centering Prayer* by J. David Muyskens. Copyright © 2006 by J. David Muyskens. All rights reserved. Used by permission of Upper Room Books.

New Year's Day—January 1

From page 17 of *Openings: A Daybook of Saints, Psalms, and Prayer* by Larry James Peacock. Copyright © 2003 by Larry James Peacock. All rights reserved. Used by permission of Upper Room Books.

January 2

From page 77 of *The Africana Worship Book: Year A*, edited by Valerie Bridgeman Davis and Safiyah Fosua. Copyright © 2006 by Discipleship Resources. All rights reserved. Used by permission.

January 3

From page 34 of *Companions in Christ: The Way of Transforming Discipleship*, Participant's Book, by Trevor Hudson and Stephen D. Bryant. Copyright © 2005 Upper Room Books. All rights reserved. Used by permission.

January 4

From page 37 of *Spiritual Preparation for Christian Leadership* by E. Glenn Hinson. Copyright © 1999 by E. Glenn Hinson. All rights reserved. Used by permission of Upper Room Books.

January 5

From page 33 of *Wrestling with Grace: A Spirituality for the Rough Edges of Daily Life* by Robert Corin Morris. Copyright © 2003 by Robert Corin Morris. All rights reserved. Used by permission of Upper Room Books.

January 6—Epiphany

From page 47 of *A Guide to Prayer for All God's People* by Norman Shawchuck and Rueben P. Job. Copyright © 1990 by The Upper Room. All rights reserved. Used by permission of Upper Room Books.

Group Study Guide

WEEK 2

Going Deeper exercise is adapted from page 17 of the *devozine Guide for Mentors and Small Groups* 9, no. 6 (November/December 2006). Copyright © 2006 by Upper Room Ministries.

WEEK 3

Going Deeper exercise is excerpted from pages 16-17 of the *devozine Guide for Mentors and Small Groups* 9, no. 6 (November/December 2004). Copyright © 2004 by Upper Room Ministries.

Closing is adapted from page 17 of the *devozine Guide for Mentors and Small Groups* 7, no. 6 (November/December 2004). Copyright © 2004 by Upper Room Ministries.

About the Author

BETH A. RICHARDSON is an ordained deacon in the Tennessee Conference of The United Methodist Church. She currently serves as editor of upperroom.org (Upper Room Ministries) and as deacon at Edgehill United Methodist Church. Beth received her Master of Divinity from Vanderbilt Divinity School in Nashville, Tennessee. Beth grew up in Oklahoma and enjoys liturgy, music, and photography. Her first Advent book was *Child of the Light*. She has contributed her writing to *Alive Now* magazine, *The Upper Room Disciplines*, and two volumes of *The Storyteller's Companion to the Bible*.